T0311178

Hatred of Sex

SERIES EDITORS · *Marco Abel and Roland Végső*

PROV
OCAT
IONS

Something in the world forces us to think.
—Gilles Deleuze

The world provokes thought. Thinking is nothing but the human response to this provocation. Thus, the very nature of thought is to be the product of a provocation. This is why a genuine act of provocation cannot be the empty rhetorical gesture of the contrarian. It must be an experimental response to the historical necessity to act. Unlike the contrarian, we refuse to reduce provocation to a passive noun or a state of being. We believe that real moments of provocation are constituted by a series of actions that are best defined by verbs or even infinitives—verbs in a modality of potentiality, of the promise of action. To provoke is to intervene in the present by invoking an as yet undecided future radically different from what is declared to be possible in the present and, in so doing, to arouse the desire for bringing about change. By publishing short books from multiple disciplinary perspectives that are closer to the genres of the manifesto, the polemical essay, the intervention, and the pamphlet than to traditional scholarly monographs, "Provocations" hopes to serve as a forum for the kind of theoretical experimentation that we consider to be the very essence of thought.

www.provocationsbooks.com

Hatred of Sex

OLIVER DAVIS AND TIM DEAN

UNIVERSITY OF NEBRASKA PRESS · LINCOLN

The University of Nebraska Press is part
of a land-grant institution with campuses
and programs on the past, present, and
future homelands of the Pawnee, Ponca,
Otoe-Missouria, Omaha, Dakota, Lakota,
Kaw, Cheyenne, and Arapaho Peoples,
as well as those of the relocated Ho-
Chunk, Sac and Fox, and Iowa Peoples.

Library of Congress Cataloging-
in-Publication Data
Names: Davis, Oliver, 1977– author. |
Dean, Tim, 1964– author.
Title: Hatred of sex / Oliver
Davis and Tim Dean.
Description: Lincoln: University of Nebraska
Press, [2022] | Series: Provocations |
Includes bibliographical references.
Identifiers: LCCN 2021035777 | ISBN
9781496230591 (paperback) | ISBN 9781496231741
(epub) | ISBN 9781496231758 (pdf)
Subjects: LCSH: Sex—Philosophy. | Sex
(Psychology) | Aversion. | Queer theory.
Classification: LCC HQ16 .D3594
2022 | DDC 155.3—dc23
LC record available at
https://lccn.loc.gov/2021035777

Set in Sorts Mill Goudy by Laura Buis.
Designed by N. Putens.

CONTENTS

PROVOCATIONS

Like democracy, sex is messy and disordering, hateable as well as desirable. While some hatred of sex is unavoidable, its intensifying exploitation by the bureaucracies of neoliberal governance must be resisted. We challenge the malignant spread of this hatred by elaborating on the following provocative claims:

Sex, defined in terms of its capacity for harm, must be redefined in terms of pleasure.

Sex is incompatible with identity and with identity politics.

Hatred of sex is enfeebling the discipline of queer studies, which finds ever subtler ways of avoiding the sexual through recourse to gender, intersectionality, affect, and attachment.

Attachment theory has intensified the hatred of sex through its parasitic destruction of Freudian psychoanalysis and the subsequent weaponization of John Bowlby's work in the traumatological clinic.

Attachment theory supplies the sex-hating template for "appropriate" forms of relating; "appropriate" is the new normal.

Traumatology's worst excesses (e.g., "satanic ritual abuse")
  are the product of fundamental flaws in the general
  approach championed by Judith Herman, which tends
  to recode benign sexual inappropriateness as abuse.
Traumatology laid the groundwork for QAnon.
By insisting that all sex is potentially abuse, traumatology
  elicits acceptance for the bureaucracies of neoliberal
  governance that would monitor us ever more closely.

PREFACE

Having been in dialogue about sex and politics for roughly a decade, we wanted to test our ideas against each other more extensively. *Hatred of Sex* is the result. The book began with an intuition—that Jacques Rancière's thesis in *Hatred of Democracy* concerning the sources of, and reactions to, democratic disorder might go a long way toward explaining the aversion to sex that we observed in numerous forms in the culture around us. We imagined a book, coauthored by two queer thinkers, that would make explicit all the things Rancière never said about sex. This project would entail not only breaking with the tacit heteronormativity that pervades French philosophy even today but also putting Rancière's political philosophy into dialogue with psychoanalysis, since it was through a neo-Freudian conception of sex that we had arrived at our intuition in the first place. *Hatred of Sex* would thus to a certain extent aim to deploy Rancière against himself, as well as to transport his ideas into locales he barely had contemplated.

Meeting on the contested terrain of queer theory, we imagined we would articulate Oliver Davis's expertise in political philosophy with Tim Dean's expertise in psychoanalysis. By conjoining these bodies of knowledge, we aspired to forge a new way of thinking about the political economies of sex. However, we realized that central to both Freud's and Rancière's thought are profound critiques of the very notion of expertise. Whereas Rancière's commitment to radical equality renders the expert a figure of suspicion rather than of unquestionable authority, Freud's commitment to the unconscious disrupts any illusion of mastery, including his own. In light of these critiques, we could not simply combine and thereby double our expertise but instead were compelled to relativize it. This book offers a dramatization of that process in thought—a *thinking-between* that is neither exactly a dialogue nor yet a synthesis of what one might take to be our respective positions.

In keeping with the Provocations book series, we have a set of strong claims to advance—about sex, pleasure, power, education, and governance. We do not make these claims in a consistently unified voice. By the same token, however, we do not stake out competing positions in order to stage a debate. Both the single unified voice and the doubling of unified voice in debate similarly presuppose a conception of coherence about which we remain skeptical. Coherence entails—in the language of psychoanalysis—a repression of what might turn out to be the most interesting ideas. Put otherwise, coherence requires forms of hierarchy inimical to equality. The authoritative statements that typify expertise depend on a performance of discursive coherence that we wish, for reasons the book elaborates, to question. Thus, we hope in what follows not to silence completely the perturbation to which, in their different ways, Rancière and psychoanalysis testify.

There is something unmistakably paradoxical about advancing a polemic that involves a critique of authoritative statements about sex. The form of our argument puts us perpetually at risk of making authoritative-sounding pronouncements about the illegitimacy of authoritative statements. However, the way we have written this book together—responding to each other without either definitive agreement or disagreement—has helped us to navigate the paradox. We differ from each other on various points, but we also differ from ourselves, and rather than glossing over our non-self-identities we endeavor to embrace this aspect of the writing process. The reader should anticipate hearing a multitude of voices, not simply a dialogue, in the pages that follow. Any authority accruing to the "authorial" voice is acknowledged here as necessarily provisional.

In a sociopolitical context where scientific expertise and even basic facts have been delegitimated via the global resurgence of reactionary populism, one wishes to reassert the legitimacy of expertise. Facts, evidence, knowledge, experience: these things matter. They do not lie beyond critique, yet neither are they wholly fungible. When, despite no experience of public service, Donald J. Trump became president of the United States—and immediately following his inauguration in January 2017 we were introduced to the bizarre notion of "alternative facts"—the philosophical critique of expertise encountered its hard limit. When falsehoods gussied up as "alternative facts" encroach upon empirical realities, the impartiality of expertise becomes ever more vital to sustain democracy. This is the context in which we are trying to think, while cognizant that nobody fully controls how their intellectual arguments may end up being used or appropriated. Rancière's political philosophy emerged from a historical context in 1960s France that, quite apart from national differences, now seems a world away from our own. And yet, even as democracy appears to wither in the relentless glare of authoritarianism, Rancière put his finger on something that remains crucial for our thinking today. Unlike Rancière himself, we engage intensively with psychoanalysis to bring out that element.

The question of psychoanalysis represents the point at which our emphases as coauthors most differ. Far from viewing psychoanalysis as apolitical or merely a theory and technique of the bourgeois individual, we treat it as complexly situated ideologically and to a certain extent as a political theory in its own right. Alert to the divergent institutional trajectories it has followed in Europe versus the United States, we engage with psychoanalysis primarily as it has developed in France, where it has greater intellectual currency and has attracted many of its best exponents and most incisive critics. We have the advantage of pursuing this engagement from the relative distance of Britain and the United States. In the opening chapter we explore the claim that Rancière's "disorder"—understood as the source of hatred of democracy—may be cognate with Jean Laplanche's "perturbation," which the latter hypothesizes as the heart of human sexuality. According to this perspective, an intransigent problem of democracy, particularly in liberal democratic states, would manifest one side of the same intransigence that impedes harmonious sexual relations.

Subsequent chapters approach this problem from the perspective of governance, analyzing how contemporary forms of power work to circumvent disorder by mobilizing psychiatric authority, among other strategies of securitization. In these coercive forms of neoliberal governance, psychoanalysis and its institutions are hardly innocent. We thus aim to treat psychoanalysis as something other than an unequivocally expert discourse, while at the same time we chart its reduction to normalizing psychology with the rise of attachment theory. Indeed, we suggest that hatred of sex became intensified when Freud's radical insights about sex were consumed from within by the parasitic project of John Bowlby's attachment theory. We argue that Bowlby supplied the implicit template for "appropriate" sexual relations, a profoundly normalizing vision that subsequently was weaponized in the traumatological clinic and widely championed by liberal-governance-carceral strands of feminism.

As with sex, democracy harbors conflicts that remain irreducible to the differences among its participants or their ideological positions. Psychoanalysis furnishes one vocabulary for describing this irreducibility but certainly not our only one. Discussing sex, we draw also on a range of conceptual frameworks developed in queer theory, and we do so at a moment when the field has retreated from both sex and theory. If queer theory began with sex—"the time has come to think about sex," Gayle Rubin declared in her 1984 essay "Thinking Sex"—then by now its focus has diversified almost to the point of forgetting that inaugural provocation. This is another sign of the problem we're trying to describe and explain. Queer theory, institutionalized in universities as the discipline of queer studies, perversely has come to instantiate the hatred of sex. We track how that has happened, suggesting that no knowledge formation is immune from defensive reaction to what makes sex difficult, and therefore none can claim full authority over it. This part of our argument involves a critical engagement with the theory of intersectionality, which has proven so influential for queer of color critique. We contend that the democratic ideal of inclusiveness, when conceived in terms of identity categories, has had the paradoxical effect of excluding sex.

The place of sex in the university—disciplinarily, institutionally, extramurally—ended up as a central topic of our discussion. We began this book before the #MeToo movement gained momentum but have engaged with its ramifications, convinced that Rancière's notion of equality holds significance in this evolving sociopolitical context. Aware of the intensity of debate around this set of issues, we are conscious that we speak as two comparatively privileged gay white men. For some readers this may disqualify us at the outset from meaningful contribution to the debate. However, we reject the identitarian assumption that ideas are reducible to their authors' social position. Such *bien-pensant* sociologism too often polices the frank exchange of views vital to democracy. The prospect of writing a book about sex at this historical moment without engaging the #MeToo movement struck us as untenable. We believe the new orthodoxy insisting that *sexual harassment is not about sex but about power* needs challenging in terms that keep both sex and power equally in view, without reducing either to the other, or to gender. *Hatred of Sex* thus aspires to build on a sociopolitical context in which something about sexual relations has become newly visible and articulable. We are not claiming that the #MeToo movement exemplifies "hatred of sex" but that #MeToo throws into relief difficulties about sex that for too long our culture and its institutions, including its universities, have been determined to overlook and now risk compounding.

We want to be clear from the outset that *Hatred of Sex* is not trying to speak about gender in other terms ("sex" rather than "gender") but instead to analyze something that discourses of gender have made harder to see. By "sex" we refer not to some mythical substrate of gender but to the conflicted pleasures of specifically human bodies. When it comes to pleasure, sex is relatively autonomous of gender. Whereas Foucault famously counterposed "bodies and pleasures" to "sex" as it serves the historical deployment of sexuality, we aim to reconfigure these terms by suggesting how pleasures are more complex than he acknowledged. Thus, for us "sex" betokens something different from what Foucault means by the term—that is, the highly complex relationship that all human beings have with their body's capacities for intense, even excessive pleasure. It is the underestimated difficulty of that relationship with one's own pleasures that prompts us to speak in terms of a distinct hatred of sex.

Sex represents not only a potential object of intellectual

inquiry but also something with which each of us has a uniquely intimate and often conflicted relationship. Unlike other subject matters, no academic research on sex is necessary in order for one to have strong convictions about it. For some audiences, any extensive discussion of sex—regardless of the claims or conclusions—qualifies as a provocation in itself. What follows is an attempt to explain, conceptually and historically, why that might be so.

Our conversations on these matters have been enlivened by a host of co-conspirators whom we wish to acknowledge here. Heartfelt thanks go out to Marco Abel, Rachel Ablow, Leo Bersani, Genie Brinkema, Antoinette Burton, Robert Caserio, Lisa Downing, Lauren Goodlad, Erin Grogan, Scott Herring, Karen Lang, Karol Marshall, Robert Dale Parker, Don Pease, Adam Phillips, John Ricco, Steven Ruszczycky, Avgi Saketopoulou, Kaja Silverman, Kirstie Simson, Ramón Soto-Crespo, David Squires, Mikko Tuhkanen, Philippe Van Haute, Roland Végső, and Robyn Wiegman. Thanks also go to the audiences who responded to parts of the book presented in lecture form at the University of Birmingham, Edinburgh University, University of Nebraska–Lincoln, and the Northwest Alliance for Psychoanalytic Study, in Seattle. Tim Dean wishes to acknowledge material support provided by the James M. Benson Professorship at the University of Illinois, Urbana-Champaign, and the head of its English department, Robert Markley. At the University of Nebraska Press, Bridget Barry has been a consummate professional throughout the process, and we appreciate her enthusiasm for this book.

Hatred of Sex

1

Hatred of Sex

I, too, dislike it.
—Marianne Moore, "Poetry"

We begin with the counterintuitive claim that sex, a source of intense pleasure, is actively hated—and not only by the puritanical among us. That which is perpetually desired may be with equal passion loathed and avoided. The claim is not merely historical, alluding to a lengthy Christian tradition of eschewing the flesh, but encapsulates a situation that is far from superseded in our secular, "liberated" postmodernity. The death of God has not abated the hatred of sex. While it may be tempting to finger those others—the uptight, repressed, or joyless—as avatars of the problem, we cannot exempt ourselves if we wish to advance a universal claim. So let us be clear that hatred of sex applies to men as well as to women, to straight as well as to gay, and to the enthusiastically promiscuous as much as to the resolutely monogamous. Hatred of sex for the libertines as for the chaste—for us as well as for "them." The problem we aim to analyze cannot be resolved by othering it, although postliberation discourse on sex and sexuality often has tried, with the best intentions, to do precisely that. What we want to get at through our titular notion of hatred of sex may be thought but not mastered or overcome. It is neither merely illusory nor simply someone else's problem.

We have not said "hatred of sex for the transgendered as for the cis" because we do not wish to be misunderstood as suggesting that trans people hate their sex. The idea that every human subject has a conflicted, non-neutral relationship to their own sexuality means that mishearing, misreading, and misconstruing what others say about sex is more common than not. For this reason, debates about sex routinely become more heated than sex itself—a situation that is complicated further by how the word *sex* typically refers to sexual difference or gender, on one hand, and sexual activity, on the other. For purposes of disambiguation we stress that our focus on sex is not primarily about gender, sexual difference, or the so-called war between the sexes. Hatred of sex is not explained by misogyny, misandry, homophobia, transphobia, or biphobia, though certainly it may manifest itself in terms of those persistent bigotries. While hatred of sex often shows its face in expressions of intolerance toward people closely associated with sex (or those imagined as having too much sex), it remains irreducible to that. Further, hatred of sex is not caused by patriarchy, capitalism, imperialism, or neoliberalism. With these sweeping gestures, we wish to clear the usual political explanations out of the way, in order to use political philosophy to think about sex—and especially people's relationship to sex—in a different way.

No doubt what may appear as most provocative about our argument lies less in its sexual content than in its claim to universality. For several decades historians of sexuality have taught us to view with skepticism any universalizing account of sex. The organization and meanings of human sexuality change over time; sex is not to be understood by grounding it in invariant physiological principles or the so-called facts of reproduction. We do not dispute this critique. Rather, we hope to demonstrate how the claim to universality is grounded instead in what Rancière calls equality, a nonidentitarian principle of universal human potential. There is nothing biologistic or unhistorical about this; quite the contrary. In the course of our argument we also aim to show how—Rancière's hostility to psychoanalysis notwithstanding—a cognate principle of universal human potential is encoded in a particular conception of the unconscious. While it is easy enough to intuit how the Freudian unconscious might lead us to sex, the link between sex and Rancière's notion of radical equality may be harder to discern. We establish this link through our reading of *Hatred of Democracy*.

A Constitutive Hatred

Hatred of Democracy, first published in 2005, intervenes in political debates specific to France, while at the same time pinpointing a conundrum of democracy that exceeds the local context. Rancière argues that democracy in its original form—government by the *dêmos* as multitude—necessarily entails disorder, since it involves everyone's participation in the practice of governing. "Democracy stirs, but disorder stirs with it," he writes.[1] Government by the multitude inevitably would be messy because it involves too many people or the wrong sort of people (the rabble), with the quantitative excess of *too many* already implying the qualitative deficit of *wrong sort*. It is this implicit judgment of *wrong sort* that contravenes the principle of equality to which Rancière is committed. With the judgment of *wrong sort*, which divides the populace into those entitled to govern versus those who are not, hatred of democracy is born. Hatred of democracy is integral to democracy because the term itself was "in Ancient Greece, originally used as an insult by those who saw in the unnameable government of the multitude the ruin of any legitimate order."[2] It bears remembering that what we typically imagine as a political ideal—democracy—was once a term of abuse. Indeed, for contemporary political theorists such as Jodi Dean, who critiques democracy as capitulating to neoliberalism, it still sometimes functions as a term of abuse.[3]

This double valence between insult and ideal is embedded in the Greek word *dêmos*, "one of the three terms that from earliest classical antiquity belonged exclusively to the vocabulary of politics."[4] The word *dêmos* designated the body of citizens constituting the polis but also, conversely, those excluded from the rights of the polis: the multitude, rabble, or crowd. What democratic political discourse calls "the people" thus has simultaneously positive and negative connotations depending on context: the people-as-sovereign—the unquestionable authority of the "American people" invoked so often in political oratory—versus the common people as rabble, or what once were known in Britain as the "great unwashed."[5] The latter, associated with disorder, tend to be viewed as undermining rather than embodying the people-as-sovereign and their democratic institutions. Rancière sets out to critique recent manifestations of this tension, the "new hatred of democracy," in which French republican elites denounce in various terms the antidemocratic impulses of the multitude. His central claim is that, even as they speak in the name of democracy, they actually despise it.

Rancière points to a feature of democracy that tends to be obscured by the more glaring problems of contemporary liberal democracies. In the United States, for example, critics focus on such things as the corrupting influence of big money; the practice of gerrymandering (whereby the boundaries of election districts are unfairly manipulated); the disenfranchisement of African Americans by various means; the cynosure of the presidency (whereby presidential elections gobble up almost all political energy); and the arcane voting system of the Electoral College (whereby those candidates who, like Donald Trump, fail to win the popular vote nevertheless can win the presidency).[6] These genuine problems that impair the representativeness of representative democracy need to be tackled and solved, as they are unequivocally bad for democracy. What Rancière puts his finger on is the more elusive problem of how the *dêmos* may be bad for democracy.

Far from deforming democracy, hatred of democracy is constitutive. The tension Rancière identifies is not exactly a problem to be solved; rather, it structures the democratic experiment itself. That experiment has been analyzed by a number of contemporary philosophers and historians of democracy in ways that illuminate Rancière's thesis. For example, in *Commons Democracy*, Dana Nelson disentangles the competing impulses that animated political life in the early American republic—between the formal impulse to consolidate power in official representative institutions, on one hand, and the "vernacular" impulse to disperse democratic power through popular involvement in communal political activities, on the other. The latter impulse, which exemplifies commons democracy, "decentralizes power and invites participation."[7] By emphasizing the distinctly communal aspects of political participation, Nelson seeks to contest explanatory narratives that rely on myths of rugged individualism and the idea that U.S. democracy was handed down from on high by the framers of the Constitution. She also aspires to recover—indeed, to revive—a long-standing tradition of vernacular (or commons) democracy in order to encourage increased political participation, beyond the rituals of voting, by ordinary citizens in the contemporary United States. Relinquishing democracy to politicians or their institutions—no matter how competent they may be—rarely solves anything.

Nelson's historical account of the dynamic social labor that produced U.S. democracy resonates with our claims here, not least because she pictures the early American political process as an ongoing struggle between centripetal and centrifugal forces. She wants her readers to grasp "a form of democratic practice that could apprehend and thrive on the tensions generated between the centripetal drive of representative government and the centrifugal energy of local practices in the democratic commons."[8] What Nelson describes as "centrifugal energy" is close to what Rancière names as democracy's "disorder"; we will advance a cognate claim that the centrifugal, disordering effects of sexuality are precisely what motivate hatred of sex. (The language of centripetal versus centrifugal remains indispensable for Laplanche's psychoanalytic theory of sexuality.) For now, we note that Rancière's point about "disordering" makes explicit something that the vocabulary of "commoning" too readily disguises, namely, the rebarbative messiness of the political process in question. When Nelson spoke in terms of "ugly democracy," her approach was closer to ours.[9] By contrast, the "common" may be an already idealized category of political analysis in that the commons serves as a refuge for the rabble. Since this difference of emphasis is important for our argument, further context may be helpful.

The early modern notion of the commons—land, resources, or labor held in common rather than privately owned—has reemerged in the twenty-first century as a central concept for not only North American theories of democracy but also Italian philosophies of biopolitics. In the work of Michael Hardt and Antonio Negri (particularly *Commonwealth*, the final volume of their *Empire* trilogy), in the political philosophy of Paolo Virno, and in collaborations between Negri and Cesare Casarino, the "common" correlates with the "multitude" as a nonhierarchized locus of political power.[10] Akin to how the concept of the common endeavors to displace the liberal opposition between public and private, that of the multitude attempts to overcome the division between "people" and "rabble" in the *dêmos*. These post-Marxist thinkers share with Rancière a basic conviction that radical change occurs primarily outside representative democratic institutions when the downtrodden mobilize as if spontaneously. It is the power of the multitude as comparatively disorganized—more precisely, as nonhierarchized—that magnetizes their attention. The leaderless groups of the international Occupy movement would be one relatively recent example.

As conceptualized by the Italian philosophers of biopower, the multitude is emphatically not the proletariat, though it may include them. Rather, the multitude encompasses those hordes of ordinary people who increasingly feel disenfranchised from political processes, whether or not they are technically citizens with voting rights. In our globalized world, with its rapidly escalating inequalities, the multitude transgresses boundaries of nation, race, party, and class, encompassing migrants, refugees, and the undocumented, as well as the precariat, the unemployed, the indigent, and the homeless. Were the term not so flattening, we might say the multitude is synonymous with the "99 percent." Part of the multitude's appeal as a category of political analysis lies in its encompassing various dimensions of disenfranchisement without recourse to the segregating logics of identity. A tacit correlative of Nelson's "vernacular democracy," the multitude is ordinary, populous, and common (in the British acceptation of that term, meaning those without rank, title, or distinction). As heterogeneous but decidedly nonexceptional, the multitude offers an additional benefit of countermanding the imperialist politics of U.S. exceptionalism. Hence, in place of a chosen people, a common multitude devoid of any unified purpose.

In political philosophy this idea of the multitude reaches back to a seventeenth-century debate between Spinoza and Hobbes that Paolo Virno characterizes thus: "The two polarities, people and multitude, have Hobbes and Spinoza as their putative fathers. For Spinoza, the *multitudo* indicates a *plurality which persists as such* in the public scene, in collective action, in the handling of communal affairs, without converging into a One, without evaporating within a centripetal form of motion. Multitude is the form of social and political existence for the many, seen as being many: a permanent form, not an episodic or interstitial form."[11] Immediately one grasps how the United States, with its founding motto of *E pluribus unum*, constituted itself in opposition to Spinoza's *multitudo*: the telos of a nation tends always to "converg[e] into a One," and the more heterogeneous its population, the more forceful its centripetal motion. By contrast with "the people" as a coherent political entity capable of self-governing sovereignty, the multitude appears as an underdog concept—one that now is having its day in the sun. Extrapolating from Hobbes's antagonism to the disintegrative picture of the polis described above, Virno argues that in the multitude's centrifugal effects lies the source of its distinctive power. What Hobbesian political theory identifies as a weakness, Italian post-Marxism extols as a strength—or at least as an untapped potential for social transformation.

And yet, even as right-wing nationalists demonize the multitude as an ungovernable horde of foreigners and idolaters ("Build the wall!"), we contend that idealizing the multitude should not be the Left's principal counterresponse. Radical politics needs to reckon with what "disorder" entails, without simply negating or, conversely, celebrating it. Hardt and Negri define "the project of the multitude" as one that "not only expresses the desire for a world of equality and freedom, not only demands an open and inclusive democratic global society, but also provides the means for achieving it."[12] Their utopianism, while appealing, sounds more than a little incongruous in our historical moment of reactionary populism. A significant difference between their conception of the multitude and Rancière's lies in his disinclination to idealize it. Rancière perceives more clearly than most that the multitude, no matter how downtrodden, remains ambiguously situated in democracy. Rather than viewing the multitude and the people as starkly opposed, then, we appreciate the multitude for its unique capacity to bring out the *rabble* in *the people*.

Bring on the Rabble

An example from recent political history captures this ambiguity. It would be plausible to claim that in the United States one version of hatred of democracy goes under the banner of the "basket of deplorables." This resonant phrase, coined by Hillary Rodham Clinton during her 2016 presidential campaign, specifies distinguishing characteristics of the contemporary rabble: "You could put half of Trump's supporters into what I call the basket of deplorables," she argued in an infamous speech. "The racist, sexist, homophobic, xenophobic, Islamophobic—you name it. And unfortunately there are people like that. And he has lifted them up."[13] Clinton's point, as valid now as then, was that Trump amplifies bigotry by giving it his imprimatur. Yet, the terms in which she made the point appeared to dismiss millions of U.S. citizens as beyond the pale. Clinton's detractors seized on the term, instantly converting it into an identificatory signifier, with those proud to be "politically incorrect" embracing their brand new stigma as "deplorable." What the Left did with *queer*, the Right has done with *deplorable*. Branded with it, they ultimately transformed it into a brand in the commercial sense. Thus, folks who never would dream of acknowledging their own racism happily announce membership in the "basket of deplorables," and they have T-shirts, hats, and bumper stickers to prove it. As with other elements of blue-collar existence demeaned by cultural elites, the deplorable became a point of pride. "Deplorable Lives Matter," reads one especially barbed logo. From a different political direction, Rancière might say the same thing.

Clinton claimed in her "basket of deplorables" speech on September 9, 2016, that racism, sexism, homophobia, xenophobia, and Islamophobia are un-American values and that the "American people" are not really like that. Those divisive, retrograde values don't define the United States. Arguably the presidential election result two months later proved her wrong, as did the entire Trump presidency. We were left with the question of just how deplorable the multitude actually is—a question that in one form or another has haunted political debate in the United States ever since. Whereas some on the Left saw Clinton as hating on the people, others protested that they *are* deplorable. Charles Blow, a prominent African American columnist for the *New York Times*, spoke for many when he insisted that "what Clinton said was impolitic, but it was not incorrect."[14]

The resurgence of unapologetic racism, misogyny, homophobia, transphobia, xenophobia, Islamophobia, antisemitism, and nativism unleashed by Trump's election victory and legitimated by his rhetoric cannot be discounted as merely working class *ressentiment*. Rampant racism and xenophobia are part of U.S. history—and undoubtedly part of its present too. Our political theories of the multitude need to confront its apparently intransigent bigotry, not just its heterogeneity and potential for mobilization. We cannot blame it all on Trump and simply move on now that he's out of office.

Conversely, any democratic commitment to equality requires that vast swaths of the populace not be written off as "deplorables," even and perhaps especially when they seem to be so. This may help to explain why Rancière predicates the political on disagreement rather than consensus.[15] How then should we distinguish a legitimate aversion to prejudice from a hatred of democracy that takes the form of deploring the rabble? What happens when the commitment to equality extends to those who hold authoritarian rather than egalitarian beliefs? Hillary Clinton's political career may be over, but the "basket of deplorables" speech raised intractable questions that are far from resolved years later. Her "impolitic" comment crystallized an issue at the heart of Rancière's political philosophy: *What do we do with the rabble?*

The question, fundamental to a system of government of and by the people, concerns the fate of democracy when the people cannot be trusted to govern or to participate responsibly in their own governance—that is, when the erstwhile dignity of the people-as-sovereign appears usurped by the chaos of the rabble. The resurgence of authoritarianism in liberal democracies, together with the global spread of reactionary populism exemplified by the unlikely rise to power of Jair Bolsonaro in Brazil or the ascendancy of Boris Johnson in Britain, makes the question ever more pressing. As with Trumpism, Brexit revealed the darker side of populism. If we ask what the 2016 referendum on whether the United Kingdom should leave the European Union taught us about democratic processes, the bifurcation of response is instructive. Quite apart from the byzantine complexities of bureaucratic negotiation, those in favor of leaving saw the referendum's result as a triumph of the popular will, whereas others regarded the whole affair as an excruciating failure of democracy. There was, however, a leftist case for Brexit, which drew on critiques of the European Union as a neoliberalist institution and thus as deleterious to democratic self-determination.[16]

As if in the spirit of *Hatred of Democracy*, Brexit compelled us to confront anew the power of the people-as-rabble. Nowhere is this more pointedly expressed than in *The Story of Brexit*, a satirical text on the politics of Britain's leaving the European Union. There, alongside an illustration of a middle-class

Englishwoman reading the newspaper in her garden, we read this: "The day after the referendum, Helen woke to discover that she shared her country with millions of simply awful people she had never met who thought the exact opposite of her about most things. Helen wonders if there could be a referendum on those people leaving instead."[17] That example of humor turns on the paradox whereby democratic processes furnish above all a fresh opportunity to discover just how appalling the multitude can be. We are reminded to our dismay that the people are revolting. Rancière's point would be that hatred of democracy manifests as contempt for the rabble, who are deemed unfit for the task of governing because they are patently unable to govern themselves. Like the deplorables, the rabble cannot be trusted even to vote in their own interests because they cannot reliably identify their own interests; they cannot identify their own interests because everything about them, right down to their basest desires, remains ineluctably disordered, capricious, and self-defeating. Insisting that the multitude requires more schooling in civic responsibility, while not wrong, misrecognizes the problem. In Rancière's account the problem is coeval with democracy, not merely an unfortunate by-product of its imperfect functioning. It is encoded in the double valence of *dêmos* as both people and rabble—a doubleness that biopolitical theories of the multitude have yet to fully confront, much less resolve.

The Antithetical Meanings of *Dêmos*

We suggest that *dêmos* belongs to the small but indispensable class of elementary terms that Freud discussed over a century ago under the heading of the "antithetical meaning of primal words." These are words that have not just multiple meanings but directly opposing meanings; it is a matter of more than lexical ambiguity or polysemy. Reviewing a brief treatise by the nineteenth-century philologist Karl Abel, Freud focuses on examples from the Egyptian language, noting cursorily that the Latin word *sacer* bears antithetical meanings of "sacred" and "accursed."[18] In what is otherwise an ephemeral book review, Freud advances a bold conceptual claim, arguing that "the dream-work's singular tendency to disregard negation and to employ the same means of representation for expressing contraries" should in fact be grasped as "identical with a peculiarity in the oldest languages known to us."[19] With a startling leap, he infers from comparatively obscure philology a fundamental aspect of the human mind's functioning. The way in which certain archaic words—such as *sacer* and, we'll add, *dêmos*—signify two radically incompatible meanings confirms for Freud a notable feature of unconscious mental life, one that distinguishes it decisively from conscious cognition. The unconscious, according to Freud, follows a logic that contains no place for negation.

It is on this basis—the absence of negation in the unconscious—that psychoanalysis poses an intractable problem for any style of thinking anchored in classical logic. Freud insists in his 1915 metapsychology paper "The Unconscious" that "there are in this system no negation, no doubt, no degrees of certainty" and therefore that primary process thinking remains "exempt from mutual contradiction."[20] From the perspective of classical logic, what Freud designates as primary process thinking hardly qualifies as thinking at all. Certainly there is little difficulty in discerning how the possibility of something meaning simultaneously its opposite and itself presents a big problem for Freudian hermeneutics. Psychoanalysis can be dismissed in toto on these grounds. What interests us here, though, is less the hermeneutic issue than the fact that Giorgio Agamben, to take a salient example, has developed the antithetical meanings of *sacer* into a systematic philosophical account of modern biopower. Invoking Freud's "antithetical meanings" essay momentarily in his *Homo Sacer*, Agamben draws out its specifically political ramifications.[21] Our point is that the very existence of such antithetical meanings holds implications not only for linguistics, hermeneutics, and psychoanalysis but also for biopolitics, democracy, and government. The Freudian unconscious, with its peculiar absence of negation, has significant bearing on politics independent of any political actor's subterranean motives or duplicity.

Rancière numbers Agamben as among the covert haters of democracy, and he certainly has no time for Freud. Nevertheless, in *Hatred of Democracy* he is doing something similar with the antithetical meanings of *dêmos*, albeit without the etymological heroics or the totalizing ambition that mark the *Homo Sacer* project. Rancière formulates the antithetical meanings of *dêmos* in the following terms:

> Popular sovereignty is a way of including democratic excess, of transforming into an *arkhè* the anarchic principle of political singularity—the government of those who are not entitled to govern. It has its application in the contradictory system of representation. But the contradiction has never killed the thing that has the tension of contraries as its very principle. The fiction of the "sovereign people" has therefore served as well as not as a linkage between governmental logic and political practices, which are always practices of dividing the people, of constituting a people that supplements the one that is inscribed in constitutions, represented by parliamentarians, and embodied in the State.[22]

The stark contrast between a sovereign and a people—between, let us say, a monarch and her subjects—persists into the democratic notion of "sovereign people" without at all resolving it. If a sovereign's absolute rights over the people are transformed in modern democracy into the people's rights over themselves as *a people* (rather than as individuals), then "popular sovereignty" retains a decidedly oxymoronic quality. Emphasizing how democracy "has the tension of contraries as its very principle," Rancière gestures to the antithetical meanings of *dêmos* as both people and rabble. Put otherwise: democracy's people are at once sovereign and deplorable, governor and *ungovernable*. Hence Rancière's insistence that political practices "are always practices of dividing the people": the people must be sorted and stratified—they must actively be made *un*equal through techniques of ordering—as a way of papering over the constitutive contradiction of democracy. The fundamental gesture of division is between those who may govern and those who must be governed, a gesture that imposes and enforces inequality.

To the extent that he is parsing the antithetical meanings of the primal word *dêmos*, Rancière is effectively thinking psychoanalytically. In saying this, we concede that our reading of Rancière is heterodox and noncanonical: the aim is to draw out implications the philosopher might be disinclined to see in his own work and thereby to extend its reach. For Freud the mere existence of antithetical meanings indexes an impersonal unconscious, a radically heteronomous logic in which contraries coexist. We need not appeal to Lacan's unconscious, structured-like-a-language—or the Lacanian establishment in France, from which Rancière wisely takes his distance—to grasp the tacitly psychoanalytic dimension of *Hatred of Democracy*. The coexistence of contraries he identifies in the "fiction" of "sovereign people" may be sufficient to justify our characterization of Rancière's thinking at this point as psychoanalytic in spirit. We do so in order to extrapolate from his account of democracy a cognate hatred of sex. The centrifugal disorder of the rabble, which motivates hatred of democracy, is the same disorder that spurs aversion to sex. If Rancière claims that contempt for democracy is built into democracy as "the government of those who are not entitled to govern," then we claim that antipathy toward sex subtends even the unmistakable joys of sex. The problem is internal to sex, as it is to democracy, and therefore cannot legitimately be glossed over by treating it as a contingent defect in an otherwise functional system.

Paradoxes of Pleasure

We began the chapter by characterizing sex perhaps too straightforwardly, as a source of intense pleasure, in order to differentiate our line of inquiry from discussions centered on "sex" as sexual difference. Now we need to consider more closely what intensity of pleasure means. For us it means that specifically sexual pleasure has—in terms highlighted by Rancière's account of democracy—"the tension of contraries as its very principle." What Freud called the pleasure principle permits a coexistence of contraries insofar as it involves the unconscious as a heteronomous logic. Phenomenologically we know that intensification of pleasure may lead to not simply more pleasure but also pain (pleasure's ostensible opposite), just as certain kinds of pain may be experienced as erotically pleasurable ("hurts so good"). An incremental escalation of pleasurable sensations beyond some quantitative threshold prompts dramatic qualitative transformations whereby pleasure tips into its contrary. In the realm of human sexuality, any secure border between pleasure and pain can be strangely difficult to locate. There is always in sex a danger that, if you are doing it right, pleasure will become too much.

Before delving into the psychoanalytic account, it may be worth recalling that it is not only Freud but also Foucault who emphasizes the nonstraightforwardness of pleasure. "I think that pleasure is a very difficult behavior," the latter remarked in a 1982 interview. "It's not as simple as that to enjoy one's self. And I must say that's my dream. I would like and I hope I'll die of an overdose of pleasure of any kind. Because I think it's really difficult, and I always have the feeling that I do not feel *the* pleasure, the complete total pleasure, and, for me, it's related to death."[23] While much can be said about these sentences, we wish to underscore the point that, since Foucault's thesis in *The History of Sexuality* tends to be taken as a rebuttal of psychoanalysis, it is significant that Freud and Foucault concur on the inexorable difficulty of pleasure, its nonobviousness.[24] For both thinkers, the basic Aristotelian conception of humans as pleasure-seeking animals provokes more questions than answers.

When Foucault claims, "It's not as simple as that to enjoy one's self," he is far from suggesting that our experience of pleasure is impeded only by social constraints or conservative morality. To view the difficulty of pleasure as a function of external limits would be to reinstate the repressive hypothesis that *The History of Sexuality* so famously critiqued. Likewise, we wish to emphasize that our thesis, even at its most psychoanalytic, does not subscribe to the repressive hypothesis: hatred of sex remains irreducible to sexual repression. Discussing sexuality in terms of the unconscious, we refer not to a repressed content but to a primary-process logic that governs this sphere of experience and permits a coexistence of contraries that conscious rationality finds intolerable. In concert with Freud and Foucault, then, we contend that something internal to its mechanism renders pleasure difficult, paradoxical, and always potentially *un*pleasurable for those troubled creatures we call human. At the root of hatred of sex lies the problem of pleasure.

Yet, ironically, it has become harder to grasp this in the wake of Foucault, because his *La volonté de savoir* offered pleasure as a solution to the problem of sex. The opposition between "sex-desire" and "bodies and pleasures" with which Foucault concluded his polemic has become so familiar, even axiomatic, that we have lost our sense of its counterintuitive strangeness:

"It is the agency of sex that we must break away from, if we aim—through a tactical reversal of the various mechanisms of sexuality—to counter the grip of power with the claims of bodies, pleasures, and knowledges, in their multiplicity and their possibilities of resistance. The rallying point for the counterattack against the deployment of sexuality ought not to be sex-desire but bodies and pleasures."[25] Improbably separating sex from pleasure, Foucault managed to make it seem intellectually naïve for scholars of sexuality to talk about sex as something people actually have. Instead, we talk about discourse, representation, practices, resignifications, deterritorializations—and our sophistication vacates sex from the picture. The difficulties of sex rather conveniently vanish into discursive gyrations. This was to some extent the overt intention of Foucault's polemic, yet it too readily plays into that hatred of sex we are trying to illuminate by reconnecting it to the problematic of pleasure.

If, in the passage above, Foucault is implicitly critiquing Wilhelm Reich and Herbert Marcuse as prophets of sexual liberation, he nonetheless writes also against Deleuze and Lacan as the Parisian gurus of *le désir*. His argument achieves its polemical power in part by declining to mention these names (the targets of his polemic would have been obvious to Foucault's contemporaries), but this leaves an impression for today's readers that "bodies and pleasures" are keywords of the critique of psychoanalysis, rather than keywords of psychoanalysis itself. The counterposing of "bodies and pleasures" to "sex-desire" permits those who have never read Freud to regard pleasure as a Foucauldean, nonpsychoanalytic category, when in fact pleasure remains among the most important and complex of Freudian concepts. Foucault's rejection of psychoanalysis for what he called its "undervaluation of pleasure" makes little sense—until one grasps that he has forgotten Freud in favor of Lacan, for whom pleasure tended to be superseded, conceptually as well as subjectively, by *jouissance*.[26] Certainly Lacanian psychoanalysis subordinates Freudian *Lust* via its dialectic of drive-desire, displacing the metapsychological emphasis to *jouissance* as that which perpetually overrides the pleasure principle. Foucault is right that with Lacan the star of pleasure fades.

But with Freud pleasure remains central to the psychoanalytic enterprise because it governs the human psyche. In the beginning, Freud claims, "the ego-subject coincides with what is pleasurable and the external world with what is indifferent (or possibly unpleasurable)."[27] Far from its being undervalued, as Foucault complains, pleasure represents an ultimate value in the Freudian account of subjectivity. And it is worth recalling that a full half century before contraceptive technologies and shifting social norms combined to detach sex from reproduction, Freud already had redefined sex in terms of pleasure. Indeed, it was his decisive wrenching of sex from its functional definition of making babies, in favor of a less naturalistic definition based on pleasure, that accounts for Freudianism's enduring appeal to some queers and a few hardy feminists. From a psychoanalytic perspective, reproduction of the species is but an occasional side effect of sex, not its purpose.

The purpose is pleasure, now to be grasped in its full complexity as including the paradoxical capacity to provoke aversion to sex as well as desire for it. Freud, endeavoring to centralize pleasure in his theory, kept bumping up against its resistance to straightforward intelligibility. "Everything relating to the problem of pleasure and unpleasure touches upon one of the sorest spots of present-day psychology," he declares.[28] Sexual activity, rather than simply reducing tension through discharge—as the psychophysiological model organized around homeostasis would suggest—actually evokes a more profound tension between "bound" and "unbound" libidinal energies. Sex evokes, in other words, a conflict between centripetal and centrifugal forces at the level of the embodied psyche, akin to how democracy evokes that conflict at the level of the political. If sex promises pleasure and contentment, it also at the same time risks generating psychic disorder for the subject of pleasure.

Disorder, a term we take from Rancière's political philosophy, finds its psychoanalytic cognates in Laplanche's *dérèglement* and *ébranlement* ("perturbation" or, as it often is translated in queer theory, "shattering"). This is the idea, in brief, of sexual intensity as psychically disturbing rather than, or in addition to, just being physically satisfying. Sex disorders us. Here the word *disorder* refers not to disease or pathology (as in a psychological disorder or a sexual dysfunction) but to the disruption of psychic coherence occasioned by sexual intensity. A fundamental paradox of specifically sexual pleasure consists in how it may be experienced as pleasantly satisfying and unpleasantly dislocating at once. Finding the paradox intolerable, our culture endeavors to resolve it by attributing the contrasting experiences of pleasure/unpleasure to the different parties in a sexual encounter, often segregating those contrasting experiences according to gender, rather than acknowledging their unsettling coexistence.

Freud's value at this juncture lies in his explicitly tackling the difficulty of pleasure. As early as 1905, in the first edition of his *Three Essays on the Theory of Sexuality*, he ponders this difficulty:

> The fact that sexual excitement possesses the character of tension raises a problem the solution of which is no less difficult than it would be important in helping us to understand the sexual processes. In spite of all the differences of opinion that reign on the subject among psychologists, I must insist that a feeling of tension necessarily involves unpleasure. What seems to me decisive is the fact that a feeling of this kind is accompanied by an impulsion to make a change in the [psychical] situation, that it operates in an urgent way

which is wholly alien to the nature of the feeling of pleasure. If, however, the tension of sexual excitement is counted as an unpleasurable feeling, we are at once brought up against the fact that it is also undoubtedly felt as pleasurable. In every case in which tension is produced by sexual processes it is accompanied by pleasure; even in the preparatory changes in the genitals a feeling of satisfaction of some kind is plainly to be observed. How, then, are this unpleasurable tension and this feeling of pleasure to be reconciled?[29]

Struggling to adjudicate how a sexual sensation can be at once pleasurable and unpleasurable, Freud is wrestling here with precisely the "coexistence of contraries" that Rancière observed in the theory of democracy. The paradox is not solved by the release of tension in orgasm because that pleasure, intensifying beyond a certain threshold, disrupts psychic equilibrium and threatens subjective coherence. What Freud will come to see, not without dismay, is that the baseline pleasure of the ego ("the ego-subject coincides with what is pleasurable") remains perpetually at odds with the more intense pleasures of sexuality. Thus, if sexual activity promises pleasure, it also threatens to generate unpleasure—not when sex fails or things go awry but exactly when sex achieves the goal of maximizing pleasure. There cannot be sex without conflict, in this psychoanalytic account, because sexually induced pleasure for one psychical system provokes unpleasure—disturbance, disharmony, disorder—for that more highly organized system of the psyche that Freud named the ego (*das Ich*). It is *I*, not the other, who dislikes it.

If it seems hyperbolic to speak of *hatred* of sex—isn't that putting the matter too strongly?—then we might consider how Freud, in "Instincts and Their Vicissitudes," aligns unpleasure specifically with hate. There he insists that, "just as the pair of opposites love/indifference reflects the polarity ego/external world, so the second antithesis love/hate reproduces the polarity pleasure/unpleasure, which is linked to the first polarity."[30] Hatred is the ego's automatic response to whatever challenges its centripetal dominance of psychic life, including disturbances emanating from that very body on whose form the ego is modeled. Those polymorphously perverse pleasures associated with the body of childhood exercise a virtually irresistible centrifugal tug on the centripetally organized yet nonetheless fragile ego or self. In this vision of selfhood as a kind of psychic armor or prophylaxis against sexuality, we glimpse the human ego exposed as something like an overworn condom.

Freud does not put it in quite these terms, of course, though his daughter led the way in redescribing the ego as an accretion of defenses, and we shall see how today the popular notion of identity serves similar prophylactic functions.[31] But first it may be worth considering how the paradoxes of pleasure, as Freud explores them, are embedded in the term he does use— specifically, the common German word *Lust*. As he observes in a footnote on the very first page of his *Three Essays on the Theory of Sexuality*, "The only appropriate word in the German language, '*Lust*,' is unfortunately ambiguous, and is used to denote the experience both of a need and of a gratification."[32] To this observation the translator James Strachey adds, "Unlike the English 'lust' it can mean either 'desire' or 'pleasure.'"[33] Thus, for example, Freud's term for the principle that he views as regulating psychic life from the start is *Lustprinzip* (translated as "pleasure principle"). A major conceptual distinction that subsequently divided Deleuze and Foucault—with the former elevating desire over pleasure while the latter inverted their values—seems utterly obviated in the German word *Lust*.[34]

Commenting on Freud's footnote, Aaron Schuster suggests that "Freud appears to have missed the opportunity here to follow his own lead as set forth in his essay 'The Antithetical

Meaning of Primal Words,' and view the ambiguity of *Lust* as a telling instance of dream-work within language, instead of just an unfortunate conceptual confusion."[35] If the German *Lust* betokens both a desire for something and the satisfaction of having it, then the word holds not merely different meanings (as many words do) but polarized meanings. Conventional notions of semantic multivalence fail to do justice to this linguistic peculiarity. As with Rancière's handling of *dêmos*, contraries coexist in both the ordinary German word *Lust* and that which it designates. The conflict within the word encrypts the conflict within pleasure itself—an irreducible tension that, since it defines sexual pleasure, can be relieved only partially and momentarily by those releases of tension associated with sex. Erotic pleasure may be curtailed in various ways by religion, morality, and social convention, but it is stymied by its own strangely antithetical dynamics, too.

Pleasure against Eros

In connecting hatred of democracy with hatred of sex, we are far from advocating a return to the notion of sex as primary causative principle. Our claim is not that one kind of hatred determines the other but rather that in their homologous structure each illuminates the other. The parallels become clearer when we consider how Freud employs a dialectic of binding-unbinding to explain the paradoxes of pleasure and the specifically human aversion to sexual intensity. The disorder of democracy, as embodied in the figure of the rabble, expresses a particular kind of "unbound" energy that necessarily threatens the coherence and stability of "bound" forms, whether those forms be political or sexual, social or subjective. Here we draw on a distinction between the mental activities of binding (*Bindung*) and unbinding (*Entbindung*) that was fundamental to Freud's thought but nevertheless quite complex, insofar as both binding and unbinding generate kinds of pleasure. If the work of binding psychic energy confers the psychological satisfaction of coherence and thereby serves to secure boundaries, then that of unbinding sparks the exhilaration of transgressing limits—including one's own—that may be especially alluring during sex. Binding functions centripetally, while unbinding does so centrifugally.

The language of binding offers a conceptual vocabulary for describing mechanisms of group formation and the establishment of social, as well as subjective, borders. Freud suggests that the pleasures of binding consist in joining smaller entities into larger wholes and thereby in creating self-contained units. Examples of bound forms would be the human ego or self; the modern political idea of the individual; the social group, community, or political party; and the nation, with its sovereign people bound together as a discretely bordered entity. Binding creates identities. Moreover, Freud claims that the work of binding generates pleasure, because it draws on the force of libido to achieve its aims. Culture, he argues, "aims at binding the members of the community together in a libidinal way . . . and employs every means to that end. It favours every path by which strong identifications can be established between the members of the community, and it summons up aim-inhibited libido on the largest scale so as to strengthen the communal bond by relations of friendship."[36] Here "aim-inhibited" libido serves the alternative aim of securing social bonds; the aim that is inhibited is the ostensibly more direct one of sexual satisfaction, for which something like social satisfaction is substituted. Instead of sex, then, we have the not inconsiderable pleasures of being a social animal and, indeed, of feeling oneself to be part of a demarcated community or group.

It is striking how, at a certain point in his account of libidinal binding, Freud invokes the Greek myth of Eros to explain this human impulse to join, to bind, and to preserve. In *Beyond the Pleasure Principle* he famously speculates that "the libido of our sexual instincts would coincide with the Eros of the poets and philosophers which holds all living things together."[37] This gesture arguably attempts to rescue psychoanalysis from its status as a suspect science by situating it closer to philosophy or poetics (a project that contemporary psychoanalysts such as Adam Phillips have pursued more deliberately). One decade later, in *Civilization and Its Discontents*, Freud refers to "Eros . . . betray[ing] the core of his being, his purpose of making one out of more than one."[38] Eros, in Freud's account, unites rather than divides. It may be worth noting that when middle-class people wish to discuss sex without being crass about it, they frequently have recourse to the language of eros. In polite society the erotic is more palatable than the sexual; likewise the genre of erotica tends to be more socially acceptable than that of pornography. Laplanche and Pontalis point to this desexualizing tendency of "the erotic" when they observe that "using the term 'Eros' risks reducing the import of sexuality in favour of its sublimated manifestations."[39] Speaking about sex in euphemisms keeps it at a safe distance, and appealing to Eros initiates preliminary steps along the well-trodden path leading to hatred of sex.

If we glimpse here a new paradox, one in which Eros appears closer to an antonym than a synonym for the sexual, then that is because sexual pleasure too readily induces the centrifugal force of unbinding. Differentiating sexuality from eros, Laplanche pinpoints the distinction in the following way: "Eros is what seeks to maintain, preserve, and even augment the cohesion and the synthetic tendency of living beings and of psychical life. Whereas, ever since the beginnings of psychoanalysis, sexuality was in its essence hostile to binding—a principle of 'un-binding' or unfettering (*Entbindung*) which could be bound only through the intervention of the ego—what appears with

Eros is the *bound and binding form* of sexuality, brought to light by the discovery of narcissism."[40] Eros, more than a classical synonym or euphemism for sexuality, enables a contrast to be drawn between manifestations of libido that bind and those that, conversely, unbind. With the term *Sexualentbindung*, Freud identifies in sex a pleasure that, far from simply joining people together à la Eros, exhilaratingly blows them apart. This notion of sexuality as strangely resistant to eros is specifically psychoanalytic; it distinguishes Freud's account of sex from more familiar, intuitive accounts.

The antagonism between sexuality and eros, emphasized by Laplanche as early as 1970, finds its way into Foucault's subsequent history of sexuality in the form of a distinction between *scientia sexualis* and *ars erotica*. Having ostensibly demystified sex as merely "an ideal point made necessary by the deployment of sexuality," Foucault was searching for techniques of pleasure that eluded capture by this modern *dispositif*.[41] Wanting an art rather than a science, he regarded Freud and his followers as too enthralled by *scientia sexualis*; in his view psychoanalysis could generate neither the longed-for aesthetics of pleasure nor a poetics of subjectivity. Yet, it is striking that a distinct tradition of French psychoanalysis as well as Foucault's own critique of psychoanalysis both counterpose eros to sexuality. If, for Foucault, eros becomes the preferred alternative to "sex" and sexuality, then for Laplanche sexuality's disquieting capacity to unbind effectively desublimates the idealization of eros. Their valuation of the terms contrasts sharply, yet they coincide in treating sexuality and eros as antonymous.

The idea of a distinctly sexual pleasure that countermands eros has led Aaron Schuster, in his book on Deleuze and psychoanalysis, to postulate "two contrasting ontologies of pleasure," which he traces back to fundamental differences between Plato and Aristotle.[42] Claiming that "Western philosophy has always been split between two paradigms of pleasure," Schuster elaborates the multifarious ways in which these competing paradigms have been described and apprehended since antiquity.[43] What is crucial for our argument is Schuster's contention that the two ontologies of pleasure remain in conflict at the level of the human subject. Without necessarily being aware of the Plato-Aristotle debate over pleasure, people experience this conflict—in their bodies and psyches—as discomforting, even excruciating.

Invoking Freud's formula for "neurotic unpleasure" ("pleasure that cannot be felt as such"), Schuster writes, "This is arguably the paradigm case of pleasure in psychoanalysis, the strange phenomenon of a pleasure that cannot be experienced as pleasurable by the ego: something in me enjoys even though I am disturbed or horrified or disgusted by it; it continues to press on and realize itself irrespective of my needs and desires, or how I feel. Freud thus turns around the standard pessimistic claim: it is not so much the lack of enjoyment that makes life miserable, but the fact that it is full, even too full, of unfelt or unenjoyable enjoyment."[44] Schuster slides, in this passage, from the Freudian problematic of pleasure to the Lacanian one of "enjoyment," using the now standard English translation for that erstwhile untranslatable French term *jouissance*. We prefer to tarry with complexities on the near side of the pleasure principle, rather than beyond it. Schuster nevertheless indicates how it is the pleasures taken in sex that provoke unpleasure for our egos that in turn permit us to speak of hatred of sex. Each and every time sexual activity offends my sense of myself—my dignity, my integrity, my identity, or my certainty about knowing what I want—the dueling paradigms of pleasure make themselves felt as an internal conflict. If Adam Phillips has rather ingeniously directed our attention to *unforbidden* pleasures, we in turn emphasize the persistent Freudian problem of *unpleasurable* pleasures.[45]

These are the challenging pleasures of unbinding, evoked by Freud in the final chapter of *Beyond the Pleasure Principle* when he asks "whether feelings of pleasure and unpleasure can be produced equally from bound and from unbound excitatory processes."[46] He replies forthrightly that there is "no doubt whatever that the unbound or primary processes give rise to far more intense feelings in both directions than the bound or secondary ones."[47] Unbound pleasures are simply more intense—so intense, in fact, that it is not always clear they are pleasurable. Their intensity approaches the borderline between pleasure and something that remains unrecognizable as pleasure *to the ego*, which is, after all, a quintessentially bound form. If, in Laplanche's terms, sexuality remains hostile to binding, then the correlative point would be that the ego is hostile to unbinding. The human ego, with its myriad defenses against disordering, is what hates sex once it reaches maximal intensity. Our culture's penchant for regarding sexual activity as an ego-enhancing pursuit, when it is treated as a conquest or as "notches on the belt," overlooks the extent to which sexual intensity also is capable of denuding the ego. Viewing sexual experience as a conquest of the other entails strenuous denials of how sex—its unbinding intensity—threatens to conquer me.

The Shibboleth of Identity

From the Freudian perspective, sex poses a problem because its pleasures promise to bind and unbind at once. Far from the antidote to hatred of sex, then, pleasure emerges as its counterintuitive source. And just as extolling the desirability of democracy entails glossing over its intractable difficulties, so the promotion of "bodies and pleasures" as "the rallying point for the counterattack against the deployment of sexuality" strategically glosses over this insoluble paradox at the heart of specifically sexual pleasure.[48] While everyone—from pundits to parents, religious leaders, college students, and "incels"—debates how much sex people are having or should be having, any discussion about how much pleasure is desirable remains conspicuous by its absence. We are suggesting that how much sex and how much pleasure are rather different questions.[49] One might be wanting more sex but less pleasure; an increase in frequency may emerge as a strategy for managing intensity via the routinization of practice.

According to this logic, the more sex you have, the less overwhelming its pleasures. Seeking sex would be a way of getting rid of it—getting rid, that is, of what makes sex psychically discomforting. The British psychoanalyst D. W. Winnicott spoke about young people's propensity for using sex to get rid of sex. Although he focused less on sexuality than did Freud—indeed, the object relations tradition performed a vanishing act on sexuality, with its effects continuing to this day—Winnicott implies that what we call hatred of sex may take the paradoxical form of pursuing sex, or certain kinds of sexual experience, as well as of avoiding it. Repetition is an attempt at mastery through binding. One expresses hatred of it by having sex in a particular way.

Rancière's cognate claim is that democratic governments use democratic institutions and processes to get rid of the *dêmos*. In one passage (quoted earlier) he insists that "political practices . . . are always practices of dividing the people." With the Freudian model in mind, we note that political practices of dividing the people operate primarily through mechanisms of binding. In other words, processes of unifying *and* of dividing "the people" function similarly. This may be because, Freud suggests, "it is always possible to bind together a considerable number of people in love, so long as there are other people left over to receive the manifestations of their aggressiveness."[50] Group cohesion requires targets of hostility outside the group yet sufficiently close to be hated. If those "left over to receive the manifestations of their aggressiveness" remain insufficiently proximate, then the libidinal mechanism falters. Freud's examples feature geopolitical entities that share a border—"the Spaniards and Portuguese, for instance, the North Germans and South Germans, the English and Scotch [sic]"—and whose populations are not in fact substantially different.[51]

Libidinal binding demarcates boundaries that thereby serve to secure borders. Thus, the popular slogans of Trumpism— "Build the wall!" "Lock her up!" "Send her back!"—all encode strong messages of division, which, by reinforcing imaginary boundaries, consolidate the libidinal cohesion of that portion of the electorate known as Trump's base. These are, in other terms, the "deplorables," whose unbound energy has been mobilized politically by positing a common enemy in comparatively close proximity, whether inside the borders of the continental United States or threatening to overrun its borders. This helps to explain why immigration, in a nation founded on it, nonetheless remains such an inflammatory issue—and so dangerously divisive in our globalized, multicultural world, where people of all races, ethnicities, and creeds need to live side by side without permanent borders. Libidinal binding, by creating what we might call fake borders, divides the *dêmos* against itself.

Here we stress that what Rancière refers to as democracy's "disorder" differs sharply from the trademark chaos of Trumpism. Trump divided the people by binding a powerful minority (the "deplorables") to himself, based less on imaginary identification than on his galvanizing of the libidinal energies of hatred. Although in almost every respect politically inept, Trump figured out how to bind to his gaudy brand some of the unbound, centrifugal energy of the multitude. Rather than serving the people, as presidents in representative democracies are supposed to, he served himself and his brand: *the base* replaced *the people* in a political calculus for which partisanship cannot fully account. Polarization, far from a contingent outcome of this individual's toxic behavior, names that mechanism whereby the centrifugal energies of the rabble are bound and exploited. If he were not constantly whipping crowds at his rallies into a fervor of hatred, or incessantly tweeting rage and bile, Trump's political power would dissolve.

Grasping how this mechanism works at the national political level helps us to appreciate why its operation at the subjective level remains so insidious. The rationale for, and result of, binding at the level of subjectivity is identity. Today identities are what bind us to ourselves and, in so doing, serve as the primary bulwark against unbinding—and hence against sexuality in the psychoanalytic sense. Identities are binding; they forge coherence out of disorder and alterity. By dividing me from not-me, identities are also exclusionary; "build the wall!" remains the implicit motto of every identity formation. Further, identities are misleading because they conceal from me my own incoherence, my constitutive dividedness, and those aspects of me with which I cannot readily identify or sympathize. Rather than an expression of diversity, identities betoken the repression of diversity.

Since identity is the first casualty of that particular pleasure Freud named *Sexualentbindung*, contemporary notions of sexual identity make no sense from a Freudian perspective. Unfortunately, this has not prevented North American psychoanalysts from trafficking liberally in such notions. Speaking about "sexual identities" has become in recent years a way of signaling one's resistance to heternormativity and indeed to all exclusionary forms of sexual essentialism. Given its deleterious history, psychoanalytic resistances to heteronormativity—and to the idea that there is just one correct developmental route to sexual maturity—are always to be welcomed. But pluralizing identity as "identities," far from ameliorating the problem, actually exacerbates it, just as multiplying defenses does nothing to mitigate defensiveness. Every identity is an imaginary formation, a province of the ego with its territorial borders. Group identities are no less defensive than individual ones; possibly they are more so. To claim that I have dual identities or intersecting identities, in the lingo à la mode, is simply to declare that my ego presides over various territories that it will defend against incursion. If identity denotes the ego's colonizing designs on experience, then narcissism could be redescribed as the imperialism of the psyche. Beneath contemporary claims made in the name of group identity, no matter how ostensibly progressive or radical, one hears the insistent clamor of narcissism.

Identities pose a special problem when it comes to sex because, as prototypically bound forms, they remain antipathetic to the effects of unbinding that characterize sexual pleasure at its most intense. Sex undoes identity. The contemporary shibboleth of "sexual identity" is, from the psychoanalytic point of view, a contradiction in terms. One cannot credit the concepts of both the unconscious and identity; they are mutually exclusive. The psychoanalytic unconscious spells the impossibility of each and every identity. In this light our cherished identities may be redescribed as desperate defenses against the polymorphousness of pleasure, the multiplicity of desire, and above all the centrifugal forces of unbinding. Trumpism has made abundantly evident that there exist no nontoxic identity formations. The psychic mechanism through which they come into being renders all identities inherently conservative.

We are well aware of the objections such claims are likely to provoke in an age when appeals to identity tend to be understood as generally liberal or progressive. No individual or group likes having their narcissism challenged—or, for that matter, having their commitment to identity described as an expression of narcissism. Learning that pride in one's political identity may amount to little more than an ego defense hardly qualifies as welcome news. For a complex set of historical reasons, we have become invested in not just our own individual identities but the very idea of identity. A rhetoric of identity—along with an array of largely covert identitarian assumptions—has colonized subjective, social, and political intelligibility: identities have become the lens through which too many people, progressive as well as conservative, view the world. We have, in the words of Walter Benn Michaels, "learned to love identity and ignore inequality."[52] Although he does not frame his critique in psychoanalytic terms, Michaels argues that the massive investment in social identities has shifted attention away from economic inequality, such that loving identity—that is, embracing a powerfully narcissistic illusion—makes other aspects of the world much harder to perceive. Identities encode strong disincentives to see outside themselves, rendering us oblivious to our commonalities, to that which we share before or beyond our manifold differences. What we share is our equality.

The Power of Equals

We are suggesting, from a different angle than Michaels, that identities obstruct equality. The way in which identities come into existence renders them antithetical to equality: the forming of any identity through imaginary misrecognition makes of one's counterpart a rival rather than an equal, in a relationship marked by struggle for domination. No other can ever be regarded as truly equal from an identitarian perspective. Yet, since people vary from each other in so many ways, we want to know in what their equality consists—what, despite our manifold differences, do we share in common? If the notion of the common, discussed earlier, helps to ground equality, then we see how equality cannot be based on property, privacy, citizenship, or, indeed, individuality. Equality, to be meaningful, must be shared by all. If it doesn't extend to everyone, it cannot hold for anyone. Although with justification we decry escalating inequalities—the widening chasm between rich and poor, or between the ultrawealthy (the "1 percent") and everyone else— nevertheless equality cannot be a matter of degrees. If you don't have full equality, then you don't have equality: it evaporates the moment some become "more equal than others," as Orwell famously put it.[53] Equality is what human beings share with one another before (and beyond) the multitude of characteristics that differentiate us from each other.

Equality therefore should be understood as the foundation from which any subsequent hierarchy is produced. Rancière, discussing the right to govern in democracy, contends that "the power of the best cannot ultimately be legitimated except via the power of equals."[54] The right to govern in democracy is contingent upon the fact, whether acknowledged or not, that anyone might exercise it. From the perspective of equality as foundational, any hierarchy must be provisional and, in the end, illusory. Democracy is formal acknowledgment in the political sphere of radical equality. But this equality remains an anti-foundational foundation, a paradoxically groundless ground for politics, because it is so utterly contingent: in democracy, "the power of the people . . . is not the power of the population or of the majority, but *the power of anyone at all*, the equality of capabilities to occupy the positions of governors and of the governed."[55] To presuppose equality implies not an even distri-bution of talents or attributes (equality is neither sameness nor a denial of difference) but an equivalence of political potential shared by all.

If in the face of radical equality we perceive existing social hierarchies as contingent rather than necessary, then we also must acknowledge that mastery and expertise can be only provisional. A psychoanalytic name for this acknowledgment is "the unconscious," a term that designates not our subterranean desires but the impossibility of self-mastery, identity, or complete self-possession. Freud qualified the idea of mastery by observing that the ego is no longer master even in its own house.[56] Equality depends on the common and, in psychoanalytic terms, on the unconscious as a condition of self-dividedness we share by virtue of being human. Adam Phillips, in a discussion of democracy that draws on Chantal Mouffe's political philosophy, argues that "the only equality that exists . . . is in each person an equality of rivenness, an equality of unknowingness, the equality born of there being no foundations to master."[57] We are all unmastered equally, though this aspect of equality is one that many progressives appear less than enthusiastic to acknowledge or accept. The implications of radical equality entail a crushing blow to human narcissism; hatred of democracy stems from what seem to be equality's unbearable inferences.

Phillips teases out the psychoanalytic resonances of equality by describing how "being equal to" someone or something suggests being able to bear them. Just as I am equal to a task if I can bring myself to undertake it, so am I equal to an experience if I am willing to undergo it. By extension, I am equal to myself—and thus more likely to be equal to others—if I can somehow tolerate my own self-dividedness and hence the illusoriness of identity. If, paradoxically, I can be at peace being at odds with myself, in an ongoing way, then I can be equal to the disagreements and conflicts that inevitably mark democratic life. "Disagreement is taken for granted," claims Phillips, in tune with Rancière; "from a psychoanalytic point of view, disagreement is itself a solution."[58] Disagreement is not what needs to be resolved for politics to proceed but "is itself a solution," because disagreement acknowledges equal yet divergent viewpoints, without subordinating one to another.

We propose that psychoanalysis offers the political sphere a unique space in which one may practice disagreeing not only with another—the analyst and whomever they may represent (one's parents, one's partner, one's boss)—but also with oneself. It is a place where I can argue with the many versions of myself without ever having to be right. In this microcosm of democracy, the analyst is an ally insofar as they assume a nonantagonistic disagreement, one in which the stakes are high but there is no expert to adjudicate. Skeptical about expertise, Freud insists that the unconscious turns the doctor into a layman; acknowledgment of the unconscious relativizes all claims to expertise.[59] No one holds the trump card, in psychoanalytic dialogue, because there is no trump card, no finalizing interpretation that would authoritatively end disagreement. The intervention of the analyst in making an interpretation can never be a question of settling the matter (*this* means *that*) but of offering another viewpoint—and, moreover, offering the humbling perspective that there always will be another viewpoint. In this way a psychoanalyst enables dialogue to continue when it threatens to stall in agreement.

Phillips underscores the following claim in Mouffe's antiessentialist account of democracy: "modern democracy's specificity lies in the recognition and legitimation of conflict and the refusal to suppress it by imposing an authoritarian order."[60] The correlative of equality in this understanding must be not harmony but a particular kind of conflict, which Mouffe calls "agonistic pluralism." If, in the French revolutionary view, equality gives rise to fraternity, then this is a fraternity of disagreement, difference, and plurality rather than of consensus, homogeneity, or identity. What holds us together as equals in democracy would be, paradoxically, our disagreement with each other rather than our shared hostility toward some outsider. Whereas polarization requires libidinal binding to achieve its baleful political effects, disagreement counters binding by forestalling the consensus of identity. Polarization functions centripetally, but disagreement does so centrifugally. Thus, disagreement (or agonistic pluralism) serves as a potential antidote rather than as a precursor to the polarizing, identity-driven partisanship characteristic of some ostensibly democratic states today.

Our identity formations, with their social media–reinforced echo chambers, make disagreement exceptionally difficult to hear. But to concede that one might be wrong and that there is much one does not know, far from betraying a weakness, acknowledges the unconscious as a universal condition of political speech and action. To concede that one might be wrong does not mean that the other guy is necessarily right but that there exist plural perspectives, other viable worldviews beyond one's own. It is too easy to resolve disagreement by one party's imposing a solution on the other, thus circumventing their equality. Striving to keep conflict alive—in part through refusing the false solutions of repression, as well as those of coercion—psychoanalysis aspires to sustain equality's viability. Considered in this light, the notorious "interminability" of psychoanalytic treatment appears as less a ruse for lining therapists' pockets than a strategy for exploring the potentials of disagreement longer than anyone dreamed possible.[61] In psychoanalysis, as in democracy, we want every voice to have its say, recognizing that there are always more voices—and more competing perspectives—than there are bodies in the room or the public square. Perpetually it seems yet another voice has something to say. If this sounds practically intolerable (why won't the dissenting voices just shut up? can't we just cancel them?), then we start to grasp what equality entails—and how the radical equality described by political philosophers such as Mouffe and Rancière (and redescribed psychoanalytically by Phillips) far exceeds formal equality before the law. What would it take to be equal to this understanding of equality, to find it bearable in an ongoing way?

Deplorable Sex

The disconcerting equality introduced by the unconscious—an equality of "rivenness" or the impossibility of self-mastery—brings sexuality back into the picture. For it is in sex that we are most prone to experiencing our rivenness as both pleasurable and distressing; the coexistence of contraries can be hard to bear. Here the claim is that sex and equality meet in the unconscious—and therefore that sexual equality cannot be conceived adequately without taking account of the unconscious as a heteronomous logic. This is particularly the case in our time of heightened inequality, when liberal culture demands, more strenuously than ever, egalitarian experience from sexual exchange. We emphasize that sex is neither the expression nor the repression of politics; it is not a complete refuge from the political nor is it simply acting out the political in another form. Given that sex involves the frictions of physiological, emotional, and psychological power, it inevitably provokes questions concerning equality. Today we want so much from sex—as if we believed that economic inequalities and their social consequences could somehow be remedied, or compensated, by achieving equality between sexual partners, equality between genders, or the equal distribution of pleasure in erotic experience. Our culture has massively overburdened sexual intercourse with expectation and freighted it with significance, including political significance.

If sex, in failing to meet our elevated expectations, so often disappoints, then this is not just another instance of human desire outstripping satisfaction. Hatred of sex betokens more than merely frustration at desire's persistent excess. Sexual experience may indeed seem hateful when it fails to yield what we want from it; however, the stronger version of this claim is that sex inspires loathing for its propensity to reproduce inequality. Beyond failing to yield the positive good of complete pleasure, sex yields a distinctly negative outcome by exacerbating social inequalities, especially those of gender, race, class, and nation. The radical feminist claim that heterosexual intercourse magnifies and consolidates women's subordination has been absorbed by liberal democracies to the extent that we now—almost automatically—affirm sex as a theater of equality. One sees evidence of this shift in the college classroom, where students routinely speak about sex as if the principal point of having it were to perform equality—as if pleasure, lust, or anything less salutary than equality of personhood and mutual acknowledgment were wholly incidental. A proving ground for autonomy, liberation, and egalitarianism, sex has become an arena for validating our modern political ideals.

This enlightened perspective on sex is broadly understood, if not always followed in practice. As a widespread liberal consensus about sex, it is simultaneously laudable and lamentable. It is laudable insofar as it suggests that a certain feminist critique has gone mainstream: the feminist project of sexual equality, while far from fully realized, has won remarkable victories. What we regret about the broad liberal consensus is that it promotes a vision of sex from which every deplorable element has been hygienically expunged. The new sexual enlightenment hinges on denial of everything that makes sex difficult—not least its unbinding intensity—as if the disordering effects of sexual experience could be eliminated by political resolve. Not only do we aspire to find the truth of who we are through sex, as Foucault argued; more improbably still, we imagine that truth should reflect positively on us and should in fact confirm our ideal versions of ourselves. These assumptions, grounded in our political ideals, render it that much harder to confront the deplorability that sex makes apparent.

"Most of what we are sexually remains impossible to communicate with anyone whom we would want to think well of us," writes Alain de Botton.[62] Articulating a disjunction between the source of our most intense pleasures and our ideal image of ourselves, the philosopher does not quite acknowledge that the person I almost always want to think well of me is myself. It is my own cherished ideals, my own sense of myself, that sex so readily violates. Sexual pleasure—specifically, its centrifugal propensity for unbinding—threatens my sense of myself as a coherent being with secure boundaries. This is what makes sexual activity so appealing but also, conversely, so off-putting. Even when my partner is doing everything right, sex risks potential boundary violations. There is some part of me—a deplorable part from which my ego recoils—that longs to have certain boundaries breached.

For example, the desire to be fucked within an inch of my life can be hard to square with egalitarian ideals. Sex may be the arena in which I do not wish to be equal but to be dominated, to embrace subservience to another. Here it is a matter not just of attending assiduously to the other's pleasure but of intensifying my own through abjection and debasement.[63] Needless to say, any desire for sexual domination—for a hand squeezing the throat, for a smack to the face, or for an insistent pushing of boundaries—violates the liberal consensus that sex should be a performance of equality. A friend who is into fisting tells us, only half in jest, that he's not satisfied "until the bedroom looks like a crime scene." With this expression, we take him to be referencing signs of disorder and, indeed, evidence of *ébranlement* (sexual shattering). Our friend is suggesting that, for it to qualify as satisfying sex, he needs human bodies to leave traces of having been affected beyond their usual limits.

But aspiring to make the bedroom resemble a crime scene sets the bar for sexual satisfaction at a uniquely disturbing level. It prompts me to question exactly how far I might go to get fucked within an inch of my life. When sex seems indistinguishable from violence, or appears as otherwise deplorable, there is a tendency to recoil. And yet, even as the ego recoils from deplorable sex, another part of us may become aroused. The longing to be fucked *within an inch of my life* implies that part of me requires extinguishing—by force, if necessary—in order that I may access properly sexual pleasure, as distinct from merely erotic pleasure. It is not that I permit the other to fuck me roughly—and then more roughly still—to maximize his pleasure but, rather, my deplorable own.

Since we insist upon equal treatment in society, employment, and law, why would we ever yearn for something so drastically unequal in our sex lives? The question is resolved by neither the liberal notion of consenting adults nor the plausible claim that we treat each other as equals outside the bedroom. One can hardly expect sexual practices that push against boundaries to stay contained within any designated space, least of all the bedroom. No small part of the deplorability we're trying to describe consists in sexuality's propensity for overrunning its allotted space. What psychoanalyst Avgi Saketopoulou calls "the escalating economy of the sexual drive" propels the quest for pleasure beyond conventional limits, whether of domestic space, physiological capacity, or psychological permission.[64] Violating the boundaries of selfhood in the service of pleasure often entails trespassing other boundaries or borders. The pleasures associated with psychic unbinding necessarily wreak havoc on bound forms.

The claim that sexual pleasure hinges on some kind of violation—psychical if not necessarily physical—may sound unconscionable to contemporary ears. No wonder people hate sex! In an attempt to forestall sex panic, we emphasize that it is not violation of the other but of myself that delivers the intense pleasures of unbinding: it is my own ego, not someone else's, whose boundaries must be at least temporarily overcome. Sex provokes extraordinary ambivalence because it may entail consenting paradoxically to one's own violation. You face the problem of negotiating boundaries not only with your partner but also with yourself. How far am I willing to go in the pursuit of pleasure? The question is equivocated when understood in terms of orgasm, since the pleasures of unbinding exceed that common physiological marker. The *petite mort* of orgasm may be the safe version of unbinding.

If we have reached the question of intensifying sex beyond orgasm, then we are well beyond functional, homeostatic, reproductive, or evolutionary conceptions of sexual activity. We may be wondering what this kind of sex looks like. The examples of fisting or getting fucked within an inch of one's life are not meant to be representative, since the thesis of *Hatred of Sex* aspires to universality. We have refrained from specifying our claims in terms of particular sex acts, and we have insisted that sexual identities always defend against the centrifugal effects we've endeavored to describe. Our argument is not about the radical potential of practices such as fisting, bottoming, or nongenital sex (delightful though those may be). Instead, we are pointing to a deplorable potential existing in all sex that approaches a certain threshold of intensity. If this sex had an orientation, it would be neither gay, nor straight, nor queer. Deplorable sex is oriented toward disintegrating the human ego and violating its ideals, including its political ideals, in the service of pleasure.

To the extent that queer theory exhibits no shortage of political ideals, sexual deplorability offends the norms of the field. We have hesitated to align the deplorable with the queer not only because "the deplorables" are associated with Trumpism but also because queer theory, as an intellectual formation, has been surprisingly squeamish about sex. Too often queer theorists seem eager to talk about anything else. An intellectual endeavor that was supposed to make sexuality a legitimate object of study for humanists and social scientists has proven far from immune to the hatred of sex. This problem exceeds the predictable—indeed, necessary—way in which academic disciplines normalize their subjects and procedures. We engage this problem in the next chapter by tracking the complex fate of sex in queer theory. The disappearing acts that queer scholars have performed on sex point to a constitutive tension between knowledge formations and sexual disturbance.

2

Does Queer Studies Hate Sex?

"The time has come to think about sex," declared Gayle Rubin in 1984, at the outset of "Thinking Sex," an essay that subsequently became canonized as a foundational text of queer theory.[1] It is one of the great ironies of the past several decades that the academic field of study Rubin helped to inaugurate ended up using the category of queer largely to forestall thinking about sex. Scholars in queer studies today generally devote their intellectual energies to something—anything—more politically palatable. "What does queer studies have to say about empire, globalization, neoliberalism, sovereignty, and terrorism?" asked the editors of a special issue of *Social Text* two decades after Rubin's salvo.[2] Setting an agenda no less ambitious than it was suffused with political gravitas, they continued, "What does queer studies tell us about immigration, citizenship, prisons, welfare, mourning, and human rights?"[3] These questions imply that queer studies, practiced responsibly, might save the world, so far-reaching is its explanatory power. (Dare we imagine the queer activist-scholar in superhero tights?) But the questions beg others: Whence the source of the global salvific potential? Why does the time for thinking sex always appear as either reassuringly past—been there, done that—or perpetually deferred to a future that never comes? How, in short, did queer studies stray so far from sex?

This chapter traces the strange fate of sex in a field that Rubin helped to inaugurate. What follows is neither a complete history of queer studies nor an evenhanded appraisal of the many scholars who have made significant contributions to it over the past three decades. Instead, the chapter follows one particular strand—that of sex—in order to assess why it has not sustained scholarly attention. We argue that the political and conceptual categories devised to "think about sex" paradoxically have fostered its eclipse from intellectual consciousness. Those categories have been articulated, disarticulated, and rearticulated in complex, occasionally contradictory, ways that we endeavor to unpack here. We focus on key arguments from the 1980s—notably by Gayle Rubin, Kimberlé Crenshaw, and Leo Bersani—that helped to set the terms for the explosion of queer scholarship and activism in subsequent decades.

Understanding the fate of sex in the university, including its intersectional articulation with "race," requires some consideration of the intellectual prehistory of queer studies. It is worth noting that this intellectual prehistory, encoded in key statements by Rubin, Crenshaw, and Bersani, stems from a comparatively broad range of academic disciplines: feminist anthropology, critical legal studies, and psychoanalytic literary theory. Even at the outset, then, queer studies drew from the humanities and social sciences, as well as from the professional field of law; its intellectual sources remain strikingly cross-disciplinary, as any serious discourse on sex must be. No academic discipline holds the monopoly on sex. As an object of study, sex has neither discipline nor home department; instead, it wanders around the university as it wanders around the body.

Frequently voiced concerns that queer studies has lost its radical edge strategically overlook how an interest in sex may be constrained by the commitment to political radicalism. One might say that paradoxically the birth of queer presaged the death of sex. In the wake of Foucault, anatomizing the political economies of sexuality—a critical procedure that involves linking sex to other systems of the social body—enabled sexuality to become the subject of serious academic research, to become disciplinarily recognizable beyond evolutionary biology. But making sex an academic subject entailed cleansing it of deplorable elements: in order to enter the university, sex needed to become at least semirespectable. Sex was enjoined to become *sexuality*, preferably of the self-contained, nonleaky, identitarian sort. In the end, however, sex became most institutionally acceptable when it could be redescribed in terms of gender and race, categories with which the neoliberal university, despite its myriad hierarchies and exclusions, is considerably more comfortable. For this process of institutional domestication, a new catalyst was necessary—and that is where *queer* became indispensable.

Rubin and the Disarticulation of Sex from Gender

The term *queer* was unavailable in 1984 as a descriptor for the "radical theory of sex" that Rubin aspired to create.[4] Having not yet been reclaimed or transvalued, *queer* was still an overwhelmingly stigmatizing term—a pejorative label—directed at lesbians, gays, the transgendered, and people with disabilities, among others. *Queer* pointed to sexual deviance but also beyond it, to other kinds of bodily infirmity, physiognomic oddity, and social nonconformity. With this category unavailable, Rubin, in constructing her "radical theory of sex," drew on a multidisciplinary array of predominantly gay thinkers, including historians (Allan Bérubé, John D'Emilio, Judith Walkowitz), sociologists (Jeffrey Weeks), and above all the philosopher Michel Foucault. At this point, Rubin was working with a minority rights model derived from the civil rights ferment of the 1960s; sexual minorities were conceived as specifically political entities along the lines of racial and ethnic minorities. Thus, even as "Thinking Sex" registers the impact of *The History of Sexuality*, Rubin was more concerned with sexually repressive laws than Foucault's model countenances, and she held fast to the language of sexual "liberation," a notion that Foucault disputed. To imagine one's sexuality might be liberated misconstrues how power operates to produce and not only to constrain sexuality; there is no "outside" of power into which one could be freed. Despite its invocations of Foucault, then, "Thinking Sex" is considerably less Foucauldean than much of the queer scholarship that followed it.

What Foucault—along with Bérubé, D'Emilio, Walkowitz, and Weeks—gave Rubin was the map of an exit route from sexual essentialism: "sexuality is impervious to political analysis as long as it is primarily conceived as a biological phenomenon or an aspect of individual psychology."[5] Rubin grasped how, in order to think about sex critically, it needs to be not only de-biologized but also de-psychologized, de-privatized, and de-individualized. Our use of psychoanalysis follows this lead, treating sexuality as something other than merely "an aspect of individual psychology": individualizing sex segregates it within the confines of identity. Rubin argued passionately for the rights of stigmatized sexual minorities, while at the same time making clear how sex and sexuality exceed the realm of individuals and their putative privacy protections. Conventional liberal notions of personhood, privacy, and individuality are insufficient for thinking sex. Retrospectively, we can view Rubin's essay as poised on the cusp of an anti-identitarian conception of sexuality that would flourish with the first wave of queer theory in the subsequent decade.

If "Thinking Sex" maps an exit route from sexual essentialism, it also pointedly marks Rubin's distance from feminism as the primary framework for conceptualizing sex. Her departure from feminism has been chief among the essay's sources of controversy, no less so in the ensuing decades than in 1982, at the famous feminist conference where it was first delivered.[6] "I want to challenge the assumption that feminism is or should be the privileged site of a theory of sexuality," Rubin announced. "Feminism is the theory of gender oppression. To assume automatically that this makes it the theory of sexual oppression is to fail to distinguish between gender, on the one hand, and erotic desire, on the other."[7] Here we have the ground-clearing distinction that enabled a new field of research—subsequently known as queer studies—to emerge, with the issue of its relative autonomy from feminism, women's studies, and gender studies perennially in question. Rubin is indispensable, in our view, for her insistence that sex and sexuality remain irreducible to the terms of gender.

Disarticulating sexuality from gender effectively displaces heterosexuality as the paradigm for sex. When taken as the normative model for sexual attraction, heterosexuality assumes that desire flows automatically between masculine and feminine; it assumes that the other's gender is, above all, what sparks lust. This model, still dominant in much feminist research, holds that desire depends on difference and that when it comes to sex what's at stake is primarily sexual difference or gender difference. Differences between genders—however they are conceived or multiplied—remain a sine qua non of feminist analysis. Rubin suggested, to the contrary, that sexuality should be understood in other than gendered terms. For example, sexual desire might be a function of generational difference; it might center on anal erotics or on activities that have little to do with gender. Following Rubin, the literary critic Eve Kosofsky Sedgwick argued that "a great deal depends—for all women, for lesbians, for gay men, and possibly for all men—on the fostering of our ability to arrive at understandings of sexuality that will respect a certain irreducibility in it to the terms and relations of gender."[8] Queer studies comes into existence with the de-privileging not only of heterosexuality but also, more subtly, of gender. Correlatively, the moment sex becomes primarily about pleasure (rather than about reproduction, oppression, or harm), feminism loses its explanatory monopoly.

Rubin's disarticulation of sexuality from gender exemplifies what the critical legal theorist Janet Halley, in her vital book on sex, calls a divergentist move.[9] It registers the limits of feminism as a comprehensive theory, emphasizing how various aspects of sexuality, including the potential for injury or harm, may make more sense outside feminist terms. Halley, like Rubin before her, wants us "to learn how to take a break from *any* hegemonic theory," and she limns the contexts in which certain kinds of feminism—particularly governance feminism—have become hegemonic.[10] Two decades earlier, Rubin had challenged feminism's near-monopoly in sociopolitical discussions of pornography. Her divergentist thesis in "Thinking Sex" grew directly out of the feminist "sex wars" of the 1970s and 1980s—a set of intense, often acrimonious debates within the women's movement over pornography, lesbian BDSM, and sex work.[11] At the heart of the sex wars was the question of sexual pleasure: who had rights of access to it, how it should be defined or regulated, and ultimately whether sexual pleasure could be compatible with feminist politics. Along with Pat Califia, Carole Vance, Ellen Willis, and others, Rubin argued that the feminist policing of erotic pleasure (including the pleasures of pornography) further oppresses already stigmatized sexual minorities; she decried the alliance of antipornography feminists (such as Andrea Dworkin and Catharine MacKinnon) with the religious Right; and she critiqued "erotophobia" in its various manifestations. It is worth making explicit that Rubin's side in the sex wars—known as "sex-positive feminism" or "pro-sex feminism"—emerged from that period of contestation as victorious; for many years it seemed to be the academic Left's default position on sex. With some qualifications, Rubin's position is where we begin *Hatred of Sex*.

As argued in the previous chapter, however, sex positivity is constrained by its tendency to require strategic elisions of deplorability. Pro-sex politics too often entails sanitizing the vision of sex being promoted. For example, BDSM is typically defended as "safe, sane, and consensual," without really acknowledging the psychic risks that constitute much of its appeal. Recognizing the paradoxes of pleasure—including that sadomasochism may be at once physically safe and psychically unsafe—complicates political advocacy for sexual pleasure. If you regard yourself as battling the repressive forces of sexual puritanism, then it is always and only the other who hates sex. In this political struggle, pleasure quickly becomes purified of its disordering elements and claimed as an unalloyed good. Thus, whenever conservative feminists denounce BDSM as sexual violence (including BDSM practiced by lesbians), the feminist counterargument tends to downplay any capacity for erotic intensity to violate the self-contained subject. The appeal of psychic violation can appear as too politically volatile to publicly acknowledge or own.

Rubin's writing remains caught in that double bind. On one hand, she was actively involved in founding and promoting SAMOIS, a legendary lesbian BDSM organization in the San Francisco Bay Area that fought feminist censorship and campaigned for the rights of sexual minorities.[12] On the other hand, the political context of the sex wars meant that defenses of lesbian BDSM seemed compelled to minimize its darker aspects. This contradictory dynamic is at work in Rubin's key concept of benign sexual variation, which rationalizes sexual pluralism by emphasizing the harmlessness of difference: "Variation is a fundamental property of all life, from the simplest biological organisms to the most complex human social formations. Yet sexuality is supposed to conform to a single standard. One of the most tenacious ideas about sex is that there is one best way to do it, and that everyone should do it that way. . . . The format of a single sexual standard is continually reconstituted within other rhetorical frameworks, including feminism and socialism."[13]

The concept of benign sexual variation entails understanding differences between sexual practices anthropologically—as value-neutral variations—rather than according to moral (or political) hierarchies that privilege one sexual form as the ideal from which others deviate. Rubin does not hesitate to call out feminism and Marxism as ostensibly radical schools of thought that nonetheless elevate one sexual form—the ideologically correct one—over others. "It is just as objectionable to insist that everyone should be lesbian, non-monogamous, or kinky, as to believe that everyone should be heterosexual, married, or vanilla," she insists.[14] The problem lies less in the content of the sexuality being promoted than in how one sexual arrangement gets privileged over others, such that the differences among them become hierarchically valued. Rubin's point is that the differences should be understood as neutral, rather than as freighted with moral significance. She helpfully redescribes deviance as pluralism. As we'll see in the next chapter, however, this understanding of benign sexual variation has been lost in the rush to combat sexual abuse, with any appreciation of benign difference overridden by invidious assumptions about harm.

For now we emphasize that the centripetalism of what Rubin calls "a single sexual standard" is connected to the recurring intellectual dream of a single comprehensive theory. Both the ideal sexual arrangement and the ideal explanatory model are imaginary formations—projections of the human ego as an artificially totalized form. Like Halley, Rubin challenges totalizing explanations, claiming that no single theory or method can parse all social phenomena. In "Thinking Sex" she develops this point via the analogy of feminism's self-differentiation from Marxism, whose totalizing ambitions failed to account adequately for gender ("attempts to make Marxism the sole explanatory system for all social inequalities have been dismal exercises").[15] In a similar fashion, she contends, feminist attempts to understand all social inequalities through the lens of gender end up short-shrifting sexuality ("feminist thought simply lacks angles of vision which can encompass the social organization of sexuality").[16] The target of the critique is less feminism per se than totalizing theories and methodologies. A nonfeminist account of sexuality, Rubin and Halley insist, need not be an antifeminist account.

Twenty-five years later Rubin offered a notably different analogy for her disarticulation of sex from gender. At a conference honoring her work, she claimed:

> The revision I suggested in "Thinking Sex," about the relationship between sex and gender, is well within the mainstream traditions of social theory. It was done in much the same spirit as Max Weber's analytic strategy for grappling with different kinds of social stratification. Weber distinguished between class, status, and party, as well as ethnicity and caste. . . . I had proposed developing the kind of nuanced distinctions for gender and sexuality that Weber applied to hierarchies of status and class. This should hardly be controversial.[17]

Weberian sociology, which made no appearance in "Thinking Sex," is invoked a quarter century later to rationalize (one might say normalize) a move whose provocativeness Rubin declines to acknowledge. But the disarticulation of sexuality from gender was, and continues to be, controversial. Rubin's move was so controversial, in fact, that the field of research generated by her disarticulation likewise refuses to fully acknowledge it. The founding of queer studies appears unsettling for many of the scholars in the field, particularly those who wish to rearticulate sexuality with gender—to heal the imaginary wound of their partial split.

Back in 1984 Rubin did not mince words. Contending that "it is essential to separate gender and sexuality analytically to reflect more accurately their separate social existence," she was quite aware that this separation "goes against the grain of much contemporary feminist thought, which treats sexuality as a derivation of gender."[18] Rubin knew she was fighting an uphill battle, yet she went further in her argument: "Sex is a vector of oppression. The system of sexual oppression cuts across other modes of social inequality, sorting out individuals and groups according to its own intrinsic dynamics. It is not reducible to, or understandable in terms of, class, race, ethnicity, or gender."[19] From the perspective of contemporary queer studies, which aspires to render sexuality comprehensible precisely "in terms of class, race, ethnicity, or gender," Rubin's claim is tantamount to heresy. How should we adjudicate these competing perspectives, both of which hail from the academic Left and, moreover, equally claim the vantage of political radicalism?[20] It is not that Rubin's thesis reveals an underdeveloped claim that queer studies subsequently fleshed out and refined; rather, her claims are antithetical to the field's methodological consensus. How did that come to be?

Crenshaw and the Intersection of Sex with Race

Rubin's divergentism came to look heretical once intersectionality established itself as the dominant approach in queer studies:

intersectionality exemplifies what Halley calls convergentism.[21] The editors of the "What's Queer about Queer Studies Now?" special issue of *Social Text*, for example, assert as axiomatic that "sexuality is intersectional"; by 2005 such claims had become the field's undisputed methodological common sense.[22] Yet, the idea that sex should be understood intersectionally is exactly the assumption we wish to dispute, by showing how identities may be intersectional but sex is something else. To make that distinction clear, we need to unpack the basic elements of intersectionality, which emerged from the field of critical legal studies during the late 1980s and early 1990s as a critique of antidiscrimination doctrine. While anthropologist Rubin focused on the harsh U.S. laws regulating sexual conduct, legal scholar Kimberlé Crenshaw focused in two key articles on the "intersection of race and sex" in antidiscrimination law and, more broadly, in the U.S. cultural imagination.[23] By thinking sex together with race more concertedly than had been done before, Crenshaw made apparent what was missing—and who was being overlooked—in U.S. jurisprudence.

It is crucial to grasp that when Crenshaw appeals to the "intersection of race and sex," in fact she means the intersection of race and *gender*. This is one of those confusing arenas in which, although sex appears to be the subject of discussion, gender is actually what's at stake. Crenshaw refers to sex because she wants to show how sexism intertwines with racism, particularly in the lives of Black women, and therefore how antidiscrimination legislation's tendency to treat racism and sexism as separate forms of bias "essentially erases Black women's distinct experiences."[24] She also refers to sex because Title VII of the Civil Rights Act of 1964 (the basis for antidiscrimination doctrine in the United States) refers to sex when it prohibits employment discrimination "on the basis of race, color, religion, sex, and national origin." Outlawing discrimination based on gender, the legislation included the word *sex* to protect women, as the statute makes explicit: "The terms 'because of sex' or 'on the basis of sex' include, but are not limited to, because of or on the basis of pregnancy, childbirth, or related medical conditions; and women affected by pregnancy, childbirth, or related medical conditions shall be treated the same for all employment-related purposes."[25] In a recent landmark decision, *Bostock v. Clayton County*, the U.S. Supreme Court extended the protection "because of sex" to include gay, lesbian, and transgender people.[26] Even in that case, however, the court's reasoning hinged on taking *sex* to mean gender. The fact that a majority conservative court extended this protection (and that Associate Justice Neil Gorsuch, a Trump appointee, authored the opinion) prompted lively debate over how radical or conservative the decision actually was. Our primary concern on this matter differs, since we wish to emphasize what gets overlooked when sex is subordinated to gender by treating the two terms as interchangeable.

Crenshaw, in contrast, is concerned with what gets overlooked when racism and sexism are misconstrued as mutually exclusive; intersectionality is the remedy she proposes to solve the problem. From our perspective, intersectionality makes certain phenomena newly visible—principally the multidimensionality of identity—but only by obscuring others. We take issue less with Crenshaw or her valuable critique than with how the intersectionality paradigm has come to dominate the field of queer studies without significant pushback. Intersectionality became central to gender and sexuality studies in the twenty-first century because it prioritizes issues of race. A growing conviction held that queer studies could overcome its reputation of normative whiteness and revitalize itself by including within its purview greater consideration of race and ethnicity, alongside its established focus on gender, sexuality, and (to a lesser extent) nationality. It would do so by showing how these categories of difference intersected—that is, by demonstrating how they are mutually constitutive rather than mutually exclusive. This effort has generated some terrific scholarship in the field of queer studies, though it also has generated a number of problems that bear on our thesis here. Intersectionality aims to combat the marginalization of certain people and the social categories they are taken to represent. However, in the process, it has unwittingly marginalized sex. Or perhaps we should say that the overextension of the intersectionality paradigm has discouraged queer scholars from thinking about sex. Thinking instead about race and gender enhances academics' political credibility and institutional authority.

Intersectionality's origins in antidiscrimination law, together with its recourse to the state for remedy, pose problems for queer studies. Appealing to the power of the state for justice and redress makes considerably more sense in the sphere of law than it does in the realm of intellectual debate. What may be accomplished in a courtroom differs substantially from what may be achieved in an academic article or book. Yet, in the quest for social justice some academics proceed as if they could harness juridical power by adopting the language of intersectionality—as if prioritizing racial justice granted them legislative capacities. Racial inequality has become so glaring and severe in the United States that many of us yearn for our research to help overcome it. We composed this chapter in the summer of 2020, after the killing of George Floyd by the Minneapolis police sparked global protests; even as we joined those protests and marched with Black Lives Matter demonstrators, we reflected on the limits of intersectionality and the too-easy conflation of academic research with political activism.

The seductive fantasy that academic work can right social wrongs has been addressed by a number of scholars, including feminist theorist Robyn Wiegman, who contends,

The success of intersectionality to secure itself as an institutionalized intellectual project arises precisely because of the transference its juridical imaginary effects in casting the state and theory as commensurate. For this reason, I would say that the present configuration in which feminist theory is read as a legislating discourse akin to the juridical state while intersectionality achieves institutional hegemony points toward two different considerations: the overreach of critical investments in the political capacities of theory and the underreach of critical attention to the contradictions and incommensurabilities of the politics of authority wielded and relinquished in diverse institutional settings.[27]

Because intersectionality originated in legal thinking, it brings with it what Wiegman calls a "juridical imaginary," which encourages its adherents to overestimate the power of their arguments about race, gender, and sexuality—as if the pronouncements of queer theorists tacitly carried the force of law. This has led to the queer-superhero-in-tights syndrome, whereby some scholars imagine they can diagnose and solve global problems ("empire, globalization, neoliberalism, sovereignty, and terrorism . . . immigration, citizenship, prisons, welfare, mourning, and human rights") with the methodologically correct queer tools. The sincere wish for a better world gives way to the fantasy of creating it by fiat, as if academic speech acts, owing to their sense of urgency, bore unprecedented performative powers. Needless to say, there is no shortage of grandiosity in imagining that academic claims might transform the world beyond the university.

The juridical imaginary of intersectionality has compounded a sense of coerciveness, or what Benjamin Weil calls "queer prescriptivism," in which queer studies aspires to legislate what scholars in the field should be thinking about.[28] If you're not working wholeheartedly on questions of race, then you obviously don't care about people of color getting killed by the police. (No one puts it quite that baldly, though hints in that direction have been dropped.) Via intersectionality, the logic of discrimination carries over from laws governing the workplace to intellectual life. Since it stems from the effort to make visible who is still marginalized by antidiscrimination doctrine, Crenshaw's account of intersectionality emphasizes how attempts to combat racial and gender discrimination paradoxically reproduce discrimination. Transposed from employment law into queer studies and gender studies, intersectionality thus licenses an intensified focus on marginalization, exclusion, and discrimination, whereby the choice to research any particular topic may be judged as prejudicial in its own right. Hence the conviction that not centering Black women in one's research actually reproduces U.S. society's marginalization of Black women.

The problem of disciplinary coerciveness means that queer studies has shifted from a critique of heteronormativity to denouncing homonormativity to either resisting or enforcing the pressures of what now is perceived as a new queer normativity. For example, the anthropologist Tom Boellstorff, building on Wiegman's argument in *Object Lessons*, cautions against what he calls "queernormativity" in sexuality studies.[29] Its institutionalization as a field of study has led to the emergence of disciplinary norms that inevitably shape research priorities, methods, and vocabularies—with intersectionality hegemonic among them, particularly in the United States. And because the field is so heavily invested in the political reach of its conceptual maneuvers, these disciplinary norms are barely recognized as such. They are seen instead as markers of political radicalism. This gives rise to a "queer prescriptivism" that, along with intersectionality, takes the form of a commitment to an impossible fantasy of inclusivity.

If it began in the late 1980s with Crenshaw's effort to show how race and gender biases converge, intersectionality since that time has expanded into what Wiegman describes an "an imperative to attend evenly and adequately to identity's composite whole: race, ethnicity, gender, sexuality, class, nation, religion, and increasingly age and ability."[30] Once the multidimensionality of identity is grasped, it readily becomes apparent that race and gender are but two of the dimensions necessary for a comprehensive accounting of social location and its variegated forms of subjectivity. To resist the pernicious politics of exclusion, one must consider as many of these variables as possible. Intersectionality thus promises "the possibility of a critical practice that never excludes"—but also a critical practice that consists in scouring the landscape ceaselessly for potential exclusions to address and resolve.[31] The fundamental democratic ideal of inclusiveness exacerbates a regrettable tendency to misinterpret feelings of being left out as evidence of motivated exclusion. To be raised in a kinship arrangement of any sort entails experiencing at one point or another the painful sense of being left out; our political discourses, both inside and outside the university, provide templates for understanding such feelings as signs of exclusion based on one's identifying features (gender, race, sexuality, and so on) and thus as discriminatory. Thinking in terms of identity thus invites paranoia on the question of inclusivity. The aspiration of infinite inclusion—which motivates intersectionality and is supercharged by it—unfortunately triggers all those narcissistic pathologies of identity detailed in the preceding chapter.

The fantasy of a methodology that never excludes is vulnerable to a more overtly philosophical critique, too. Approaching intersectionality from a feminist perspective inflected by ordinary language philosophy, Toril Moi argues that Crenshaw's method exemplifies "an extreme case of the craving for generality."[32] Moi takes the phrase "craving for generality" from Ludwig Wittgenstein, who laments a tendency, widespread among intellectuals, "to look for something in common to all the entities which we commonly subsume under a general term."[33] This is a problem in the way that we characteristically think. Developing a claim that resonates with both Rubin's and Halley's critiques of totalizing explanations, Moi suggests that Wittgenstein "is targeting a specific intellectual *attitude*, namely the constant search for the kind of explanation that brings all particular cases under *one* concept or *one* theory."[34] What gets slighted in this approach are the particular cases, which can seem of interest only insofar as they illustrate the general rule or term. For Moi the problem lies not in the existence of cases that do not fit but, rather, in the misbegotten effort to create a general rule or category that would include them all.

Although Crenshaw devised intersectionality to recognize the distinctiveness of Black women's experience, paradoxically it has morphed into a project to account for all axes of difference under its singular rubric. As Moi characterizes the problem, intersectionality aspires "to establish a complex understanding of identity, one that aims to subsume all possible kinds of identities under itself. Such a theory of identity will always be an expression of the craving for generality. In its effort to achieve an understanding of identity that excludes no one, such theories often reach fantastic levels of abstraction."[35] Abstraction becomes a problem when the response to any particular example reflexively hunts for what that example supposedly "excludes." The assumption that an example somehow should stand for all possible cases—and therefore that particularity must be interrogated for its hidden exclusions—rests on an impossibility and is politically self-defeating.

If intersectionality has been the subject of cogent critiques from within feminism (notably in the work of Wiegman, Moi,

Jennifer Nash, and Jasbir Puar), then by contrast queer studies seems to have swallowed it whole.[36] Intersectionality suited the purposes of queer scholars who wanted to displace the focus from sex to race, or those who wished to redefine queerness invidiously in racialist terms. Roderick Ferguson's recent work exemplifies this problem. His book *One-Dimensional Queer* (2019) argues that queer liberation began intersectionally, in 1969, but over time narrowed its multidimensional politics to a one-dimensional focus on sexuality. Ferguson's title plays on Marcuse's *One-Dimensional Man*, though he sometimes treats "queer" as if it were synonymous with "gay," when the whole point of queer, as it emerged around 1990, was to offer an alternative to identity-based conceptions of sexuality and to promote coalitional politics. That particular history, discussed further below, vanishes in Ferguson's account. Instead, drawing on Crenshaw's use of the term "multidimensionality" as an occasional synonym for "intersectionality," he employs the figure of one-dimensionality to align "sexuality" with whiteness, conservative politics, capitalism, and the state.[37] By overcoding sexuality in this fashion, *One-Dimensional Queer* quietly launches an ideological smear campaign against sex. Ferguson wants to foreground race by stabilizing sexuality as conservative and making sex politically uninteresting.

Needless to say, writing sex out of the picture of queer liberation entails significant historical distortions. For example, Ferguson claims that "the Stonewall riots [were] a major event in the history of intersectionality"—never mind that Stonewall occurred a full twenty years before Crenshaw coined the term.[38] Anachronisms notwithstanding, Ferguson's basic point is that the Stonewall riots, and the political ferment that fueled them, involved people of all genders, races, and classes. The historical fact that Stonewall drew on the energies of antiracist political organizing usefully broadens our sense of this chapter in the history of sexuality by making it part of the history of intersectionality too. It's worth remembering that Stonewall was not an event of gay white men only. The trouble is that Ferguson uses this perfectly valid point to elide the significance of sex and sexuality altogether.

Sex disappears from Ferguson's account of queer history within the first few pages. Consider the following synopsis: "This book attempts to show how intersectional and multidimensional queer struggles (i.e. ones that addressed the overlaps between differences of race, class, gender, and transgender) were key ingredients of that refusal" of the status quo.[39] Here the term "multidimensional queer" signifies differences of race, class, gender, and transgender, whereas "one-dimensional queer" (the bad version of queer) signifies sex and sexuality. For Ferguson, race, class, and gender edge sexuality out of the equation, lending a cover of political reputability for his refusal to acknowledge the significance of sex. From our perspective, Ferguson's thesis exemplifies the sanitization of queerness that his book ostensibly critiques. In the contemporary neoliberal university, using race to displace sex betokens a new politics of respectability. Race and gender designate matters of concern about which North American universities solicit a virtually incessant discourse. However, only in the drastically circumscribed form of identity categories or as an index of harm are they willing to hear about sex.

Crenshaw was forthright that her methodology concerns identity categories. "Because of their intersectional identity as both women *and* of color within discourses that are shaped to respond to one *or* the other, women of color are marginalized within both," she insists.[40] Crenshaw intervened in U.S. identity politics to show the complexity of identity, its multidimensionality, rather than to challenge identity as the basis for political intelligibility. Likewise, Ferguson argues for recognizing the multidimensional character of political struggle based on categories of social difference (race, class, gender, transgender, and sexuality as a function of identity). These are entirely legitimate yet severely limited projects. We have no wish to narrow the multidimensional to a single dimension but instead seek to highlight what remains inassimilable to intersectionality because of resistance to identity. Sex is not one-dimensional, an erroneously privileged component of identity, but other-dimensional. When sex means something other than gender, it becomes extremely hard to see through an intersectional lens because it occupies none of the dimensions on which Ferguson (following Crenshaw) focuses. And since it belongs on none of these dimensions, perhaps we should not be astonished that Ferguson has so little to say about sex.

Our claim is that its juridically derived emphasis on identity categories substantially constrains the intersectional paradigm's capacity to think about sex, particularly those aspects of sex that have no truck with identity. The juridical imaginary is capable of thinking sex only as gender, on one hand, or subordination and harm, on the other. Intersectionality's origins in antidiscrimination jurisprudence thus encourage attending to the convergence of racial and sexual violence; for example, when Crenshaw turns to sex, she concentrates on rape.[41] This aspect of sex is comparatively easy to discuss, in the sense that we all oppose rape, just as we all oppose racial and gender discrimination. What is harder to discuss—and neither the law nor the juridical imaginary is much help—are questions of pleasure. While intersectionality critiqued the compounding of gender subordination by racial subordination, a different strand of proto–queer theory in the late 1980s confronted the paradoxical pleasures derived from *being* subordinated. If Crenshaw was trying to liberate vulnerable populations from social subordination, conversely Leo Bersani urged us to embrace our sexual subordination.

Bersani and the Identification of Sex with Masochism

It likely has not escaped the reader's attention that our thesis in *Hatred of Sex* closely resembles that of "Is the Rectum a Grave?," Bersani's classic essay from 1987, with its famous opening sentence, "There is a big secret about sex: most people don't like it."[42] Bersani's account of sex had a strong impact on the emerging field of queer studies, even as many synopses of the field have conspicuously overlooked it.[43] One might go so far as to say that refusals to acknowledge Bersani's thesis tacitly confirm its power through their avoidance of what he identifies as aversive about sex. "Is the Rectum a Grave?" brings sexual deplorability into the conversation with renewed urgency by focusing on gay male sex during the first decade of the AIDS pandemic. Bersani asks us to regard men getting fucked in the ass—and loving it—at a moment when such acts were considered a death sentence. Although he focuses on a particular example, Bersani also extrapolates from gay men's bottoming some broader insights about sex and our aversion to it. Without claiming that gay men are representative of everyone, his argument moves from a specific sexual act to an ontology of the sexual as masochism.[44]

"Is the Rectum a Grave?" may be read as the primary intellectual manifesto of the AIDS pandemic during the 1980s. That context is worth underscoring. It is coincident with, yet distinct from, the feminist sex-wars context out of which Rubin wrote "Thinking Sex" and the women-of-color feminist context, with its civil rights legacy, out of which Crenshaw developed her theory of intersectionality. All of those struggles contributed to the emergence of queer politics during the late 1980s and early 1990s. Intense political activism around HIV/AIDS ensued from the extreme nature of the situation, in which there was no effective treatment for HIV disease and people (especially gay men) were dying at mortality rates seen in wartime, all while the president of the United States refused to acknowledge publicly that any of this was happening. Since AIDS was construed as a disease of gay men, it unleashed a secondary epidemic of homophobia, such that those who were most vulnerable became fresh targets of social hatred. It may be hard to imagine (or remember), nearly four decades later, just how feared and despised gay men were during this time. "Is the Rectum a Grave?" began as a review of Simon Watney's 1987 book *Policing Desire*, which documents the virulently phobic construction of AIDS and gay men in Britain and the United States. In light of the evidence Watney assembles, "the only *necessary* response," Bersani wrote, "is rage."[45] An extraordinary political passion animates Bersani's argument, just as it spurred ACT UP, Queer Nation, and other instances of queer activism that exploded during the early years of AIDS.

Given this ferment of political activism, it is worth asking why Ferguson never considers AIDS or ACT UP in his history of post-Stonewall queer politics. How does intersectionality facilitate that particular silencing? Since silence around HIV/AIDS helped the disease to spread unchecked among African American communities, should intersectionality engage with what some might regard as predominantly men's issues? When discussing "Is the Rectum a Grave?" in a recent course on sexuality, one student exclaimed, "I love how intersectional this essay is!" Uttered with the earnestness typical of undergraduates, this comment, it turned out, was meant to gloss the fact that Bersani mentions factors of gender, race, and class alongside his primary discussion of sexuality. Intersectionality has become a buzzword to denote the liberal value of hyperinclusiveness.[46] But "Is the Rectum a Grave?" is far from an example of intersectionality. Rather, the political milieu that forms the essay's context is one of queer *coalition*, based on the counterrecognition that AIDS is not a disease of identity. It is not a "gay disease"—even though the initial cluster of mortalities was identified in 1981 among a cohort of young gay men (in New York and Los Angeles) and, during those early years, gay men were the Western demographic most visibly affected.

There is an important difference here. Intersectionality drew on civil rights discourse, which grants recognition and protection on the basis of identity categories. By contrast, the queer politics that emerged from AIDS stresses the distinction between identity and practice that was central to Foucault's histories of sexuality. Against the homophobic construction of HIV/AIDS as a "gay disease," early queer activists insisted that it is not who you are but what you do that makes you vulnerable to infection with HIV. The emphasis falls on risky practices (unprotected sex, sharing needles) and thus contributes to the ongoing effort to help destigmatize certain populations. When, early in the epidemic, researchers spoke of the "4-H risk groups" in which mortalities were appearing—Haitians, hemophiliacs, homosexuals, and heroin users—the heterogeneity of the demographic categories already suggested that imaginary borders of identity were not going to protect anyone.[47] The politics responding to AIDS could not be gay identity politics but needed to be coalitional; queer emerges during this time as a concerted critique of identity.

Drawing on the early mobilization around AIDS, "Is the Rectum a Grave?" mounts a strong critique of identity politics by articulating an incompatibility between sexual intensity and coherent selfhood. Bersani anticipates the various queer critiques of identity poised to appear on the horizon, while also keeping sex in the foreground (eight years later, in *Homos*, he would lament the evasive desexualizations of what in the interim has become queer theory). According to his account, sex remains indispensable thanks to its potential not for liberation, as in the standard gay argument, but instead for prompting aversion ("most people don't like it"). Hyperaware of Foucault's critique of the repressive hypothesis, Bersani takes care to distance his position from the psychoanalytic model of repression: "I'm interested in . . . a certain *aversion*, an aversion that is not the same thing as a repression and that can coexist quite comfortably with, say, the most enthusiastic endorsement of polysexuality with multiple sex partners."[48] Aversion to sex is not explained by prudishness. Even as he distances himself from clichéd notions of sexual repression, however, Bersani suggests that the liberation movements of the 1960s and 1970s failed to obsolesce the Freudian theory of sexuality altogether. Despite everything—and in the midst of AIDS—Freud still has his uses for those stigmatized by sex. "Is the Rectum a Grave?" thus initiates a post-Foucauldean deployment of psychoanalysis in the service of radical sexual politics.

To appreciate the wily way in which Bersani does this, it helps to compare "Is the Rectum a Grave?" with "Thinking Sex." Rubin and Bersani, while invoking many of the same key thinkers (Foucault, Weeks, Kinsey), diverge notably in their treatment of antipornography feminism. The feminist antipornography ideology of Dworkin and MacKinnon embodies the position Rubin critiques: "A great deal of antiporn propaganda implies that sadomasochism is the underlying and essential 'truth' toward which all pornography tends," she argues. "Porn is thought to lead to s/M porn which in turn is alleged to lead to rape."[49] Practitioners of sadomasochism become scapegoats in feminism's war on pornography.

Curious about sadomasochism from another vantage point, Bersani takes a different tack. He finds Dworkin's and MacKinnon's denunciations of pornography illuminating for almost exactly the reason Rubin finds such denunciation false, namely, its characterization of routine heterosexuality as essentially sadomasochistic. Putting a perverse spin on Dworkin's and MacKinnon's erotophobia, Bersani argues that "their indictment of sex—their refusal to prettify it, to romanticize it, to maintain that fucking has anything to do with community or love—has had the immensely desirable effect of publicizing, of lucidly laying out for us, the inestimable value of sex as—at least in certain of its ineradicable aspects—anticommunal, antiegalitarian, antinurturing, and antiloving."[50] If Rubin redescribes deviance as diversity, Bersani contrariwise welcomes the deplorability of sex, pursuing rather than negating just those qualities that make sex resistant to social redemption. He thus takes the hardcore feminist critique of sex as crypto-sadomasochism—as an engine of inequality—in an entirely new direction.

By way of a very un-American reading of Freud filtered through Georges Bataille and Jean Laplanche, Bersani extrapolates from the feminist critique of sexual subordination the counterintuitively "strong appeal of powerlessness, of the loss of control" in sex.[51] If we grasp the allure of sex as an arena for relinquishing mastery—there can be no orgasm without at least temporary loss of control—the idea of *powerlessness* as appealing nevertheless goes against everything we have been taught about autonomy, agency, personhood, dignity and self-respect, and so on. Powerlessness appears profoundly unappealing politically. The "appeal of powerlessness" also runs counter to the ego, to what it means to have a strong sense of self—and therein lies its significance. Bersani is trying to explain not only why a masochistic position may be irresistible to some folks (for instance, those who love bottoming) but also how it might be tempting for anyone. Tracing a line of argument in Freud's *Three Essays on the Theory of Sexuality*, he aspires to universalize masochism—to redescribe it not as deviance, perversion, or kink but as the beating heart of human sexuality. From this perspective, the point of sex would be not just to come but to come undone.

His term for this coming undone is "shattering," a word he uses to translate those effects of the sexual that Laplanche groups under the rubric of *ébranlement* or *dérèglement*. What Bersani takes from Laplanche's reading of Freud is the insight that "sexual pleasure occurs whenever a certain threshold of intensity is reached, when the organization of the self is momentarily disturbed by sensations or affective processes somehow 'beyond' those connected with psychic organization."[52] The political relevance of ostensibly private sexual pleasure lies in its threat to the defensive coherence of the ego. Linking shattering to masochism, Bersani continues as follows:

> On the one hand Freud outlines a normative sexual development that finds its natural goal in the post-Oedipal, genitally centered desire for someone of the opposite sex, while on the other hand he suggests not only the irrelevance of the object in sexuality but also, and even more radically, a shattering of the psychic structures themselves that are the precondition for the very establishment of a relation to others. . . . Freud keeps returning to a line of speculation in which the opposition between pleasure and pain becomes irrelevant, in which the sexual emerges as the *jouissance* of exploded limits, as the ecstatic suffering into which the human organism momentarily plunges when it is "pressed" beyond a certain threshold of endurance. Sexuality, at least in the mode in which it is constituted, may be a tautology for masochism.[53]

Among the implications of this key passage are the following. If shattering betrays "the irrelevance of the object in sexuality," then by the same token it also suggests the comparative insignificance of gender to our most intense pleasures. Without an object—without, that is, "the person from whom sexual attraction proceeds"—sexuality of this type renders gender secondary at best.[54] Freud's "line of speculation" about self-shattering significantly reorients his account of sexuality away from heteronormativity. Implying gender's secondariness in sexuality also enables Bersani's analysis to resonate with Rubin's and Halley's claims concerning the limits of feminism.

Because Bersani's focus on gay anal sex displaces the normative heterosexuality that pervades discussions such as Crenshaw's, he also is able to extrapolate some political implications of sexual subordination that would be considerably harder to articulate within a feminist paradigm. If Crenshaw wants to complicate identity as intersectional, Bersani wants to shatter the boundaries of identity altogether, in order to challenge what he calls "the sacrosanct value of selfhood."[55] This entails navigating the paradoxical pleasures of subordination rather than automatically resisting them in the name of political agency. Confronting social hysteria about gay sexuality during the early years of the AIDS epidemic—a hysteria that intensified the misogynistic and homophobic perception of receptive anal sex as feminizing, disempowering, even self-annihilating—Bersani suggested that, rather than struggle to demystify such views as pernicious ideological constructs, we might instead embrace the potential for certain experiences of pleasure to overwhelm the self and temporarily inhibit its egoistic lust for power. The possibility that sex unmans should be pursued, not repudiated, he contends.

If sexual intensity violates ego defenses, then that violation could be exploited for its potential to thwart what in the previous chapter we described as the routine imperialism of everyday narcissism. In sexual pleasure there lies a violation that militates against sexual violence. The capacity of sex to violate—to "shatter" the self—could be rethought (rather than simply resisted) for explicitly feminist purposes. It is crucial to grasp how, in this psychoanalytic account, sexual intensity holds the capacity to violate oneself, not the other. This is where Bersani ends his argument in "Is the Rectum a Grave?": "If sexuality is socially dysfunctional in that it brings people together only to plunge them into a self-shattering and solipsistic *jouissance* that drives them apart, it could also be thought of as our primary hygienic practice of non-violence."[56] Sexual self-shattering holds a prophylactic value that stems from its counterintuitive tendency to break, rather than cement, interpersonal relations. (This insight forms the basis for what has come to be known as the "antisocial thesis" in queer theory.) While Bersani merely gestures toward shattering's potential to inhibit interpersonal violence, feminist and queer scholars in his wake have elaborated that insight in remarkable ways.

Earlier we mentioned that an influential strand of queer studies—the one growing out of Crenshaw—has ignored or dismissed Bersani, because the challenge that sexual self-shattering poses to ego identities is radically incompatible with the identity politics of intersectionality. However, several queer thinkers have taken Bersani's intervention seriously enough to elaborate his concept of shattering in the context of racialized subjects. What we find especially valuable about the work of Kathryn Bond Stockton, Darieck Scott, Nguyen Tan Hoang, Mary C. Foltz, and Avgi Saketopoulou (among others) is their capacity to think the politics of race without allowing the urgency of racial injustice to obscure the difficulties of sex or the conflicted appeal of ego-shattering pleasures. This scholarship, varied as it is, shares a determination to *embrace* erotic debasement (Stockton), abjection (Scott), bottomhood (Nguyen), excrement (Foltz), and the experience of being sexually overwhelmed beyond the limits of consent (Saketopoulou).[57] As with Bersani, these thinkers are not interested in redeeming sexuality or reconstructing self-mastery; like us, they remain alive to the nonredemptive possibilities of deplorability. The hard lesson—and the perennial challenge—of this set of approaches lies in grasping how "the value of sexuality itself is to demean the seriousness of efforts to redeem it."[58] That includes the power of sexuality to demean efforts to redeem it for political purposes.

The scholarship to which we're referring makes evident that Bersani's psychoanalytic paradigm is not for-gay-white-men-only, as some have claimed. It is facile to invoke the identity location of this particular critic to dismiss his argument or discount its relevance for people of color. Stockton, Scott, and Foltz amply demonstrate how the possibilities of pleasure-in-debasement are legible in African American literature—in the writings of James Baldwin, Toni Morrison, and Samuel R. Delany, among others—well before Bersani appears on the scene. Those possibilities attain a new level of intensity in the explosive theatrical work of Jeremy O. Harris, particularly his 2019 Broadway production *Slave Play*, which strongly suggests that no gender, race, or sexuality remains immune to the erotic appeal of powerlessness.[59] Irrespective of how secure we feel in our gender and racial identifications, we never can be sure exactly how we are taking our pleasures, and this is why sexuality cannot rest on the same analytic axis as categories such as gender, race, or class. Sexual pleasures, in their capacity to unmaster us, perpetually risk derailing all those political trajectories that depend on stable foundations. As Rancière says of democracy, sex is disordering, since it involves insuperable elements of deplorability that go beyond masochism and affect us all. The capacity of sex to unbind and thereby unmaster, while it may be expressed in gendered or racialized terms, remains irreducible to those terms alone.

André Green and the Degenitalization of Sexuality

Our account of how the field of queer studies symptomatically forgot about sex has nudged discussion back into the orbit of psychoanalysis—an orbit from which many of the field's practitioners have wished, for one reason or another, to free it. Depending on your perspective, sexual liberation sometimes can appear as tantamount to freedom from Freudian ways of thinking about sex. Freud has been used, particularly in the United States, to normalize and discipline sexuality. Here we need to bear in mind that it is not only queer studies that largely forgot about sex; the field of psychoanalysis began to retreat from sex in the direction of ego psychology and object relations during Freud's own lifetime. Far from being an unequivocal solution to the problems we've identified in the drift of queer studies, psychoanalysis is also part of the problem. This chapter's final sections endeavor to describe how critical discourses on sexuality seem condemned to repeat a pattern of going astray from the disturbances of sex via multiple strategies of normalization. Central to this normalizing process is the ongoing effort to circumscribe sexuality and stabilize its boundaries. Psychoanalysis contributes to that disciplinary project of stabilization in no small measure, even as Freud fatally undermines it by degenitalizing sexuality.

The psychoanalytic theory of the unconscious makes sexuality exceptionally labile. Freud learns from his patients that virtually any part of the human body, including internal organs, may become libidinally invested, such that the genitals appear, from a psychoanalytic perspective, as comparatively incidental. Complex psychical processes of eroticization—of libidinal investment—are necessary before genitalia become sites of potential pleasure. The ostensibly familiar idea of erogenous zones speaks to the possibility that nongenital areas—mouth, anus, rectum, nipples, toes, armpits, ears, behind the knees, the skin of the back—may likewise become susceptible to erotic pleasure. These nongenital regions of the body, Freud notes, appear "to be claiming that they should themselves be regarded and treated as genitals."[60] By way of the unconscious, with its propensity for displacement, Freud moves sex around the body, revealing myriad contingencies involved in genitalization. Sex disorders and reorders human anatomy. Despite popular misconceptions about Freudianism, psychoanalysis in fact deprioritizes the genitals, with the theory of shattering as one consequence.

But as we've insisted all along, Freud does not deprioritize sex. His redescription of subjectivity instead makes sex much harder to locate. The impressive range of possible erogenous zones is really the least of it, since Freud extends libido beyond the human body to inanimate objects and abstract entities. Consider, for example, the visceral responses prompted by a national flag—one of which might be defensive outrage at the suggestion that this venerable symbol could be viewed as a target of libidinal investment. Enlarging our conception of sex beyond the genitals raises a set of questions that admit no easy answers. Where should the line between sexual and nonsexual be drawn? What if we were to concede that one of the most prominent characteristics of the sexual lies in its propensity for muddying lines, trespassing boundaries, and ruining formal integrity? The problem with Freud is not that he sees sex everywhere but that his theory of the unconscious makes sex infinitely harder to delimit.

"A psychoanalytic conception of sexuality," André Green contends, "is thus distinguished from all others because it encompasses non-manifest forms—forms which are unconscious, repressed, disguised or transformed—of a sexuality which extends far beyond its observable incidences."[61] We turn to Green at this juncture because, like Laplanche, he offers a major account of retreats from the sexual within the increasingly heterogeneous field of psychoanalysis itself. Freud's extension of sexuality to "non-manifest forms" by way of the concept of libido implies that he is handling sex in the speculative domain of the nonempirical and unquantifiable. "Non-manifest forms" of sexuality require a hermeneutic operation before they can become legible as sexual, and this too invites skepticism, especially in a world increasingly doubtful about the hermeneutics of suspicion. Freud makes sex simultaneously easier and harder to see—easier to discern in nongenital sites and scenarios, but at the same time it becomes harder to fathom where sex ends and the legitimately nonsexual begins. His degenitalization of sexuality, which seems so promising from an antiessentialist perspective, provokes real epistemological problems. The recourse to sex/gender norms in psychoanalysis may be a symptomatic response to not only the disturbance of sex but also the aporias opened by degenitalization. Here sex/gender norms represent more or less desperate strategies of binding in the service of localization. In order to be socially managed, sex needs to be confined, bound, and (in Deleuze's terms) reterritorialized.

This conflicted dynamic is exemplified in the work of relational psychoanalyst Muriel Dimen, who recognized the disordering potential of sex early on but kept recuperating it in terms of gender. "Sex is extraordinary because it bridges adult and child," she insists. "In women and men alike, it juxtaposes the reality-orientation of maturity with the fantasies of infancy. It mixes the rational distinctions made by adults between self and other, mind and body, with the boundlessness of infantile feeling."[62] Although she appreciates how sexual pleasure unsettles our rational distinctions by evoking boundlessness, Dimen almost immediately relocalizes disorder in the genitals: "Representative of the ultimate contradiction of life and death, the vagina and, by extension, the female body, come to signify all disorder."[63] Gender and genitalia serve, in Dimen's account, to reestablish familiar boundaries through a rather conventional kind of symbolization (binding); the defamiliarizing psychoanalytic insight about the lure of unbinding ("boundlessness") thus evaporates. This loss of the Freudian concept of unbinding within contemporary psychoanalysis signals a pervasive problem. Too often appeals to gender are employed to tacitly re-genitalize—and thereby make recognizable—sexuality.

We suggest that Freud's radical degenitalizing of sexuality represents his version of Rubin's disarticulating of sex from gender. Although expressed in markedly different terms, it signals the same fundamental operation, one in which sexuality is detached from anatomical determinism, from the exigencies of reproduction, and above all from "observable incidences." While often (though not always) one may determine the gender of persons by seeing them—and sometimes their sexual identity too—sexuality never can be discerned just by looking. Anyone's relation to pleasure remains invisible to observers (including ethnographers or expert interviewers) because it remains at least partly obscure even to themselves. We have stressed that sexuality operates at the level of the unconscious in a way that gender, race, and class do not. But we also wish to register that sexuality can be expressed in terms of those categories, owing to their greater visual intelligibility. Gender (or race) may make sense of that which fractures sense, even as it thereby conceals the difficulty.

The lability of sexuality—its capacity for displacement—generates problems that Green describes thus:

> In no case can the sexual be understood in a way that would free it from its relations to the non-sexual, no doubt because its capacity to form connections, in diverse registers (with another drive-force, with an object, with the ego, with the cultural) is at once its inherent characteristic and proof of the extent of its power. This is what is unacceptable to the opponents of psychoanalysis. It gets in the way of any clear vision of what sexuality, in itself, actually is.[64]

Green suggests that sexuality actively resists being bound and localized: the sexual, in its propensity to form connections with the nonsexual, paradoxically blocks "any clear vision of what sexuality" is. And if this is "unacceptable to the opponents of psychoanalysis," it is also without doubt unacceptable to many psychoanalysts too. The difficulty of circumscribing sex makes it potentially anathema to the field of psychoanalysis itself. If, as we claimed in the previous chapter, sexuality is hostile to binding, then that in turn provokes hostility toward sex on the part of all who identify with the mission of maintaining boundaries, keeping things safe, and helping to make sense of the world (that includes psychoanalysts). One might say that the therapeutic profession has become obsessed with boundary violations—therapists seducing their patients—because it has lost sight of the sexual by reducing it to the genital and to the terms of gender. North American psychoanalysts are forever putting sexuality in its place (which frequently entails putting it out of mind).

By contrast, Freud insists on finding sexuality in unexpected places. Indeed, he claims, "all comparatively intense affective processes, including even terrifying ones, trench upon sexuality."[65] Whereas later psychologists such as Silvan Tomkins develop accounts of affect as a *substitute* for sexuality, Freud suggests conversely that every affective process encroaches on sexuality ("*auf die Sexualität übergreifen*") once the affect reaches a certain pitch of intensity.[66] If an affective response is sufficiently intense, then something sexual is triggered, precisely because sexuality's unwavering characteristic, no less than its ultimate aim, is intensity—or what Saketopoulou calls the experience of overwhelm (and Bersani calls shattering). When subjective coherence is threatened, a specifically sexual excitation begins to form. The counterintuitive model Freud proposes is one in which sexuality precipitates from objects and experiences that ostensibly have nothing to do with sex:

> The sexually exciting effect of many emotions which are in themselves unpleasurable, such as feelings of apprehension,

fright or horror, persists in a great number of people throughout their adult life. There is no doubt that this is the explanation of why so many people seek opportunities for sensations of this kind, subject to the proviso that the seriousness of the unpleasurable feeling is damped down by certain qualifying facts, such as its occurring in an imaginary world, in a book or in a play.[67]

Aligning sexuality with those "unpleasurable pleasures" discussed in the previous chapter, Freud is exploring some further implications of degenitalization. Affects and emotions, understood here as not fully separable from sexuality, in fact "trench upon" sex. Particularly striking in this passage is the suggestion that sexual excitement may be provoked by aesthetic experience—not because aesthetic objects contain sexual meanings that require hermeneutic decipherment but because the affective responses they generate, if sufficiently intense, may lock onto sexuality. As Laplanche once put it, "newly formed sexuality seems able to take as its point of departure *absolutely anything*."[68]

The retreat from these radically challenging ideas about sexuality started very early in the history of psychoanalysis, with Carl Jung, Melanie Klein, and the development of the British object-relations school, among others. Whereas Anna Freud pushed psychoanalysis in the direction of ego psychology, Klein diverted it from sexuality in a different direction. In Kleinian psychoanalysis, "any reference to pleasure has disappeared," laments Green.[69] For his part, Laplanche argues that Klein converts the principles of binding and unbinding (both of which concern pleasure) into the countervailing forces of love and hate, such that "what ultimately loses any real place with the antagonistic pairing of love and aggression is sexuality."[70] Laplanche underscores his objection to Klein thus:

"As with the Freudian conception of Eros, the sexual becomes totalizing, synthesizing love."[71] The condition of possibility for specifically sexual shattering vanishes in Klein's model of the psyche, and what emerges instead, via the synthetic force of love, is the key concept of reparation—a notion with which the most stringently desexualized versions of queer studies have become quite enamored.

Klein appears in the later work of Sedgwick as inspiration for methods of reading ("paranoid" versus "reparative") that have become tremendously influential in queer literary studies in the United States.[72] When Sedgwick proposes reparation as a reading method, it is in response to what she regards as the paranoid interpretive protocols of the "hermeneutics of suspicion," which came to dominate literary critical method during the latter decades of the twentieth century.[73] In other words, she was reacting to the influence of Freudian hermeneutics, particularly the idea that every text has an unconscious—a latent content or a hidden agenda—that it is the critic's job to expose. With that model of the text, literary criticism would prove its political bona fides through triumphant gestures of unmasking; ideology critique works most effectively in the realm of aesthetics when it combines Freudian hermeneutics with strains of Marxism to postulate a political unconscious.[74] And while this critical approach proved remarkably durable, it tended to feed illusions of mastery via the act of demystification: critics always knew better than the author or text. Although her audience was largely unfamiliar with Kleinian psychoanalysis, Sedgwick's critique gained traction because she articulated a growing concern with how variants of the hermeneutics of suspicion were functioning as techniques of dominance and control. Her claims dovetailed with a number of subsequent theses (including Bruno Latour's) that have been broadly influential across the humanities and social sciences.[75]

The appeal of reparation, in this context, was that it offered a promising alternative to "paranoid reading" as a technique of domination. What has come to be known as the "reparative turn" in queer studies prioritizes kinder, gentler interpretive protocols; it discourages the urge to dominate one's object of study, preferring more equitable and reciprocal object relations between critic and text. For Sedgwick, as for Klein, the reparative holds no place for the libidinal. And doubtless this elision represents a large part of its appeal to contemporary scholars. If there is pleasure involved in "reparative reading," it is largely that of imagining oneself as politically or ethically righteous vis-à-vis the objects of study—in other words, an ego pleasure. The deplorable is completely othered in a frenzy of virtue signaling, and it sometimes feels like one is witnessing among practitioners of "reparativity" what Klein called "manic reparation," a primarily defensive response to the perceived loss of critical omnipotence.[76] For contemporary queer studies, the reparative thus offers the defensive advantage of obscuring the sexual and its difficulties. The reparative turn—a turn away from sex in the direction of binding—facilitates the normalization of queer studies in the contemporary neoliberal university.

Within and beyond queer studies, the reparative turn has been amplified by a major cross-disciplinary turn toward affect. After poststructuralism, with its emphasis on language and discourse, academics yearned to bring the body, with its emotional knowledge and clamorous affects, back into the critical conversation. What is most striking about the multidisciplinary effort known as the "affective turn" is how completely drained of libido the body of affect theory appears. It is a body crisscrossed by markers of gender, race, class, age, and ability, susceptible to a range of affective intensities, yet singularly devoid of sex. If pleasure may be categorized as an affect, it is nevertheless rarely deemed worthy of consideration among affect theorists; often mentioned, pleasure is never theorized as such—perhaps because it retains the odor of Freudianism. Certainly the affect theory that develops from Deleuze inherits his distaste for pleasure as a significant concept ("I can scarcely tolerate the word *pleasure*").[77]

The version of affect theory that developed in the United States via the psychology of Silvan Tomkins was explicitly designed to escape a Freudian conception of the body. Tomkins views Freud as having "smuggled some of the properties of the affect system into his conception of the drives," an error that the former's prioritizing of corporeal affects will correct.[78] A major purpose of the Tomkins model is to downplay, delegitimize, and otherwise circumscribe sex, in favor of bodily affects understood as biologically innate. Thus, when Sedgwick—who promoted Tomkins alongside Klein as would-be lodestars for queer studies—writes, "I'm rather abashed that *Touching Feeling* includes so little sex," her expression of dismay strikes a false note.[79] The absence of sex is a feature of the Tomkins affect theory, not a bug. As the intellectual historian Ruth Leys characterizes that theory, "for Tomkins the affects are discrete, inherited, self-rewarding or self-punishing responses of the body that can be and, in the early development stages, are activated by innate triggers."[80] What Tomkins shares with Klein is an assumption about innateness (affects for Tomkins, fantasies for Klein) that utterly forsakes Freud's insights regarding libido, pleasure, the unconscious, and the constitutive difficulties of sex. An affect theory that stems from Tomkins's psychology delivers a pre-Freudian body for which sex cannot but be nugatory. One can't help wondering why scholars in queer studies, a field ostensibly committed to antiessentialist conceptions of embodiment and desire, lapped it up so avidly.

In view of these developments, we want to stress the distinction between affect theory's *desexualizing* of the body and Freud's *degenitalizing* of sexuality. Whereas Freud makes sexuality harder to pin down or circumscribe, affect theory makes it disappear, like a magic trick. This is the difference, in Laplanchean terms, between unbinding sex from the genitals and binding it very tightly so as to limit its significance. However, the distinction is complicated by what Foucault in his late work refers to as the "desexualization of pleasure."[81] This phrase, which could be translated as the "*degenitalization* of pleasure," introduces an ambiguity into an important discussion of sadomasochism. Invoking "our good friend Gayle Rubin," Foucault argues,

> The idea that s&m is related to a deep violence, that s&m practice is a way of liberating this violence, this aggression, is stupid. We know very well what all those people are doing is not aggressive; they are inventing new possibilities of pleasure with strange parts of their body—through the eroticization of the body. I think it's a kind of creation, a creative enterprise, which has as one of its main features what I call the desexualization of pleasure. The idea that bodily pleasure should always come from sexual pleasure as the root of *all* our possible pleasure—I think *that's* something quite wrong. These practices are insisting that we can produce pleasure with very odd things, very strange parts of our bodies, in very unusual situations, and so on.[82]

The notion of producing pleasure with "very strange parts of our bodies" implies generating erotic pleasure with nongenital parts of our bodies. This discussion of sm makes the most sense when one understands Foucault to be using "sexual" as a synonym for "genital": sm practices move pleasure around the body akin to how Freud's speculative theory moves pleasure around the body, such that genitalia become neither the primary nor the exclusive sites of pleasure. Here it must be reiterated that, in the psychoanalytic account we've been elaborating, "sexual" is decidedly not a synonym for "genital." Further, violence is less securely located on the side of aggression than Foucault apparently would like to imagine, insofar as Freud's degenitalization of sexuality produces a sense of the sexual as that which shatters the ego and violates the boundaries of identity. Foucault, in desexualizing pleasure, is not only degenitalizing it; he is also purging pleasure of its potential deplorability. For Foucault, as for others in his wake, pleasure emerges as an unalloyed good.

Going Astray

Our brief survey of recent developments is not meant to suggest that Kleinian or other object-relations schools of psychoanalysis lack value. Quite the contrary: redescriptions of psychoanalysis are vital to psychoanalysis. What we're trying to emphasize, by outlining how the development of psychoanalysis as a field involves retreating from the sexual, is the pervasiveness of that problem we call hatred of sex. The problem is embedded in ways of knowing and in their institutionalization as clinical or academic disciplines. This is to some extent a consequence of the strangely intimate relationship between knowledge and sex—as in that bygone era when to "know" someone served as a euphemism for sexual relations with them. Both Freud and Foucault consider the peculiar intimacy between knowledge and sex to be far from superseded. In a section of *Three Essays on the Theory of Sexuality* titled "The Sexual Researches of Childhood," Freud describes the emergence of a "will to know" directed principally to sex: "The instinct for knowledge in children is attracted unexpectedly early and intensively to sexual problems and is in fact possibly first aroused by them."[83] Here sexual curiosity appears to serve as the prototype for intellectual curiosity. No doubt it is significant that Freud, writing out of a culture that invented the research university, uses the term *research* (the noun *Forschung* in the phrase *die infantile Sexualforschung*) to characterize this childhood activity.[84] Calling it research is a way of taking seriously what others might dismiss as childish experimentation or inappropriate, even delinquent, behavior.

It is worth considering why most, if not all, children appear as sex researchers but so few adults do. One answer to that question would involve observing how knowledge as a form of mastery serves as a defense against the disordering potential of sex. The "will to know" is counterbalanced, and sometimes augmented, by an equally powerful will *not* to know.[85] If the search for knowledge is inspired by sexual curiosity, knowing (and knowingness) can nevertheless guard against the capacity of sexual pleasure to unmaster or otherwise overwhelm its subject. Hatred of sex is therefore not necessarily mitigated by knowledge or education but in fact may be fueled by either or both. As Foucault argued in the first volume of his *History of Sexuality*, the "will to know"—particularly as it manifests at the level of population—functions above all to contain and control.

We have connected various strategies of containment with Laplanche's thesis about the binding of sexuality by narcissism and have suggested that identity politics represents a scaled-up version of such binding. Localizing sexuality through binding always serves as a strategy for controlling it, at whichever scale or dimension is operative. Laplanche has proven additionally useful to our argument about the forgetting of sex in queer studies because his account of sexuality includes the idea of "going astray" (*fourvoiement*), a term he raises to the level of a concept as a sign of its pervasive significance. "There is a covering up of sexuality and the unconscious in Freud's own work," he suggests, "that parallels the covering up of sexuality and the unconscious in the human being."[86] Laplanche discerns a pattern in which discourses on sexuality, including Freud's, symptomatically forget the sexual in favor of its bound libidinal forms. By focusing on key moments in the intellectual prehistory of queer studies—moments at which sex becomes a direct object of critical thought—we have endeavored to show how the dynamic described by Laplanche works at a disciplinary level. The covering over of sex is the work not of one or two scholars but of entire modes of thinking and styles of sense making. Paradoxically, the category of queer played a decisive role in how the covering over of sex became institutionalized in the neoliberal university (queer is the deplorable redeemed). We have suggested further that the linked categories of gender and race have been conscripted to that covering over, thanks to the widespread appeal of intersectionality. Claiming not that any one of these categories is more fundamental than the others, we have instead argued for recognizing the specificity of the sexual and, indeed, its irreducibility to more readily apprehensible terms. While the "going astray" that Laplanche describes may be to some extent inevitable, it takes historically distinct forms in different contexts. The next chapter considers how contemporary bureaucracies of governance increasingly exploit our reactive tendency to bind the disturbances of sex into safer, more "appropriate" forms.

3

Securing the Appropriate

Attachment Theory Reconsidered

> *The concept of security is not enough to raise civil society above its egoism. Security is, rather, the* assurance *of its egoism.*
> —Karl Marx, "On the Jewish Question"

In *Hatred of Democracy* Rancière reminds his readers that hating democracy is "as old as democracy itself": Plato decried democracy as the pursuit of "people's pleasure for its own sake" and as "a style of life that is opposed to any well-ordered government of the community."[1] Rancière suggests that his contemporaries' "hundreds" of books denouncing the pleasure-seeking individualism of French democratic society at the turn of the twenty-first century are updated versions of this ancient hatred, with "a few modern accessories."[2] The age-old expert business of hating democracy can be understood, he argues, as an attempt to "ward off an impropriety pertaining to the very principle of politics."[3] Hating democracy tries to cover over the foundational impropriety of politics—that political power is always "the power of those who have no natural reason to govern over those who have no natural reason to be governed."[4] Thus democracy, in Rancière's radical understanding, scrambles any principle of appropriateness according to which group would be qualified to rule by virtue of its members' knowledge, experience, training, wealth, birth, age, and so forth.

In this book we are adapting Rancière's argument to suggest that the hatred of sex is likewise as old as sex itself, that hating sex accompanies sex and seeks to cover over something vital about it: a foundational impropriety upon which rest all attempts to comprehend what is sexually appropriate. We suggest that this scrambling messiness of sex can never be entirely covered over by hating it—or for that matter by trying to love it. There will always be something awkward, intractable, gauche, upsetting, and disturbing—what was once called queer—about sex that cannot be entirely sanitized within a regime of safety and appropriateness, however benign or coercive. Like democracy for Plato, sex is a destabilizing force that tends to undo individual and social ordering. Because hating sex is something we are all prone to do, this is an especially lucrative domain for those experts who teach us how to hate and whose *scientia sexualis* is encoded in bureaucracies of governance that promise security by monitoring the appropriateness of sex.

Hatred of sex as we encounter it today is an intensified, optimized form of Gayle Rubin's "sex negativity." Writing in the early 1980s, she envisaged "sex negativity" as the strongest of five "ideological formations" exercising their "grip on sexual thought": sex negativity is the conviction that sex is a "dangerous, destructive, negative force."[5] Whereas Rubin considered the sex negativity of "Western" cultures to be a lingering but potent legacy of Pauline Christianity's belief in the inherent sinfulness of sex, what we are calling hatred of sex is now actively and incessantly reproduced in the cautionary tales of moralizing experts from across the political spectrum, experts whose wary words summon a proliferation of anxiogenic bureaucracies of risk to teach the potential dangerousness of all sex. Hatred of sex thus describes the following: (1) something all sexual beings do spontaneously but that can be intensified by the cautionary influence of expert claims-makers and their models of happy intimacy; (2) the strong consensus that has developed across the political spectrum since the 1970s that sex is a danger, especially to women and children; and (3) the product of bureaucracies of risk that instantiate and reproduce hatred of sex by regulating all sex as though it were potentially dangerous.

Victims, Feminisms, and the "War on Sex"

This chapter and the next address all three of those dimensions. We aim to show how the hateable originary impropriety of sex constitutes both an affront to and an opportunity for the dominant form of administering power today, which calls itself "governance" and which organizes and benefits from the hating of sex.

Governance is not synonymous with governing but rather designates, as Wendy Brown has argued, neoliberalism's "stealth revolution," which is the ongoing antidemocratic takeover of political, cultural, and social life by practices of business management premised on narrowly functional considerations of efficiency.[6] Governance is management of the people, without politics. The radical feminist critique of liberal or "governance" feminism, to which our discussion is indebted, uses the term "governance" in a related but not precisely equivalent fashion, whereby governance refers primarily to the state in its repressive function. Thus, in Janet Halley's critique, liberal feminism's consensus around protecting vulnerability and honoring victimhood has inadvertently consolidated stereotypes of a subordinated femininity and strengthened the punitive state at precisely the moment when neoliberal reforms have withered the welfare state.[7]

According to Elizabeth Bernstein's related concept of "carceral feminism," the demand for protection and punishment by liberal feminists has strengthened and relegitimated the state's exercise of punitive and repressive functions far beyond the sphere of sex crime.[8] Arguably the Right has always wanted more punitive forms of criminal justice; yet, as Marie Gottschalk notes, during the period 1973–2006 there was a fivefold increase in U.S. incarceration rates, with Left-liberal feminisms being instrumental in establishing "a powerful elite consensus in favour of the carceral state."[9]

In a further extension of this radical line of critique, Sarah Lamble has suggested that the demands of "carceral queer" for enhanced punishment of homophobic violence and for the criminal sanctioning of "hate speech" have been similarly complicit in strengthening the repressive state.[10] Dean Spade has further argued that liberal feminism's implicit alignment with affluent middle-class values has gone hand in hand with an indifference to "the seemingly banal administrative systems that govern everyone's life, but have an especially strong presence in the lives of poor people," particularly trans people of color.[11]

Spade's concerns about unequal distributions of "administrative violence" and the unintended consequences of liberal-governance-carceral feminism are reflected in a collection of essays edited by David Halperin and Trevor Hoppe: *The War on Sex* (2017). Focusing mainly on the U.S. domestic arena, they suggest that despite significant emancipatory advances in the field of sex and sexuality over recent decades—including the availability of contraception and abortion, the development of LGBT rights, and the recognition of the true extent and real damage of sexual violence—alongside these welcome advances, a countervailing movement they call the "war on sex" has quietly set about its work. Sketching the contours of this covert "war," Halperin notes that as of December 2015 some 843,680 U.S. citizens were officially registered as sex offenders. However, very few of these are "violent sexual predators" (as few as 1 percent), and, indeed, a quarter of them are minors aged eleven to seventeen, with 16 percent of those minors being under twelve years old.[12] Registration as a sex offender lasts a lifetime and imposes onerous constraints, including residency requirements and the obligation in some states to have the fact of registration recorded on official documents such as driving licenses, as well as the obligation to report on a regular basis to the local police station and for the sex offender to pay for advertisements in local newspapers whenever they move to a new area.

Despite the evidently punitive effects of these sex offender registration and notification provisions, in 2003 the U.S. Supreme Court ruled that they were administrative rather than punitive measures, thereby exempting them from the Eighth Amendment's protection against cruel and unusual punishment, as Judith Levine notes.[13] Other essays in the volume object to the use of so-called "civil confinement" procedures, based on dubious risk assessments, to keep offenders locked up for life as psychiatric patients even after they have served their sentence—measures that the Supreme Court also ruled are administrative. As Laura Mansnerus bluntly puts it, "Some men in indefinite confinement would be better off if they had simply killed their victims."[14]

A related facet of this war on sex is the imposition of disproportionately harsh punishments, often for victimless or statutory crimes where no real harm has occurred; while rates of incarceration in the United States have fallen slightly since the economic crisis of 2008, the proportion of the imprisoned who are sex offenders has continued to rise.[15] Because of the extraordinary measures elaborated to contain them—measures that bend the law by setting aside constitutional protections to please the prevailing public mood—the sex offender is seen to be a "harbinger," as Roger Lancaster puts it. "Sexual fears and strategies for the containment of sexual dangers are key threads of the new reticulum [of social control]. They figure prominently in ongoing redefinitions of norms of governance. They provide a reusable template, suitable for application in other domains. If we want to see what social control could look like over the course of the twenty-first century, we should look to the sex offender."[16] In this respect the sex offender resembles the terrorist: a category of supercriminal against whom "administrative" measures of preventative detention can be deployed, thanks in part to the extreme social opprobrium mobilized by the label. As with the terrorist, nobody in mainstream politics and few even in critical academia will want to be seen to "touch" the sex offender, for fear of becoming contaminated by their pollution. Whereas other types of criminal have been variously humanized in the public imagination and the mass media, even murderers (thus limiting the usefulness of the once stigmatizing category of "the criminal"), sex offenders and terrorists today occupy an altogether more extreme zone of opprobrium and can readily be abjected, policed, and imprisoned without arousing public sympathy.

We broadly concur with these critiques of liberal-carceral feminism and liberal-carceral queer. However, it is less the state, or particular states, that concern us here and more the administrative technologies that undergird neoliberal governance, or the way these bureaucracies are stoked by the *scientia sexualis* of expert discourse and by narrowly framed political activism. Our claim is that once-principled liberal-feminist activism against sexual abuse and sexual violence has been co-opted by the antidemocratic project of "governance," which is hollowing out liberal democracies "termitelike."[17]

Such narrowly framed liberal activism plays into the hands of governance's promise of ever-increasing functional efficiency and consolidates its extension of a form of competitive individualism that eats away at the fabric of our social, cultural, and political life. Activism demanding of particular authorities that they investigate more effectively and punish more harshly designated categories of sex offenders, without regard for the wider considerations of social justice or the unintended consequences of improved efficiency in this one area, is no longer acceptable from the perspective of radically egalitarian social justice. When officials and politicians accede to activist demands to guarantee more sexual safety, this move tightens the hold of bureaucracies of risk, which construct all sex and all subjects as potentially dangerous in a way that appears to justify the unending expansion and intensification of these very matrices of control.

Whereas Brown had already voiced concern in the mid-1990s about the way in which too exclusive a focus on "legal 'protection' of a certain injury-forming identity discursively entrenches the injury-identity connection it denounces," our concern is less with the legal or discursive reinscription of injured identity than with its reinscription today in technologies of governance that supposedly operate within the general frame of the law but whose administering effects in fact precede and exceed the law.[18] In other words, self-optimizing bureaucracies of governance and the experts who stoke them with their dubious *scientia sexualis* are now constantly—retrospectively and preemptively— vigilant for injured identity, which represents an opportunity to curate forms of victimhood and to demonstrate that ever more extensive governance of human thought and action will always be required.

The #MeToo movement is the latest example of liberal feminism's fifty-year entanglement with victimology. Philip Jenkins describes as "historic" Florence Rush's 1971 presentation to the rape conference of the New York Radical Feminists, suggesting that it may have been "the first recorded occasion in which a presentation on sexual abuse began with a recounting of a personal history of victimization."[19] While radical feminists campaigned throughout the decade to gain wider social support for their justifiable conviction that the crime of rape was a terrorizing mainstay of patriarchy—in the process forging tactical alliances across the political spectrum with social and religious conservatives who did not find "patriarchy" remotely problematic but who had always vehemently hated sex and could readily agree that it, along with many other domains of social existence, should be more vigorously policed—the carceral-security state stood poised to reap considerable side benefits from this campaign.[20]

One year after Rush's historic presentation, the annual National Crime Victimization Survey began in the United States, and many other countries followed suit later in the decade. Such surveys do not simply measure a population's fear of crime but materialize it as an object of political deliberation that is preconstituted to call for a repressive response, embroiling politicians in a competition to outdo one another with ever more coercive measures to prove to the electorate who is better able to guarantee their security. These surveys help instantiate the liberal paradigm of security, according to which the first duty of government is to guarantee the security of the governed and the prime justification for governing is security.

Whatever precisely security means here, it is *not* economic security, for which citizens under neoliberalism are more than ever individually responsible. As Kristin Bumiller has argued, while much of the feminist mobilization around sexual violence in the 1970s was necessary, demands for "more certain and severe punishment for crimes against women . . . resulted in a direct alliance between feminist activists and legislators, prosecutors, and other elected officials promoting the crime control business."[21] Of course for many liberal feminists not only were such alliances not a problem, they were a welcome outcome of activism. However, expansion of the carceral state is something we should all be concerned about, in particular when it involves not only introducing by cross-party consensus extremely coercive measures of indefinite detention that bypass constitutional protections but also the official disavowal of the coercive reality of these measures, which are made out to be merely "administrative."

By 1977 the tactical alliance between feminists and evangelicals against rape had expanded to include medical professionals who in the preceding decade had become aware of the extent of "child battering" to create "a perception that all American children were sexually at risk"; from around 1977 "the nascent problem called *child sexual abuse* gradually appropriated the generic term *child abuse*, and a cascade of works about abuse, incest, and sexual exploitation reached flood proportions by 1984."[22] As Jenkins notes, protecting the security of vulnerable women and children—particularly against sexual violation and particularly when proposals for new laws are named to memorialize victims—has very wide electoral appeal and meets little effective opposition.[23] The cycle of competitive outbidding on security that this consensus fosters helps to explain the worst excesses of sexually violent predator legislation in the United States in the 1990s, which rightly preoccupy many contributors to *The War on Sex*.

There is more to be said about the lucrative expert business of curating victimhood under neoliberalism and the specific role that traumatological theorizations and therapies play in this, as well as the collateral benefits that bureaucracies of governance draw from the polarizing simplification of all social action into predation and victimhood. But first we wish to close this brief evocation of #MeToo by insisting, contrary to some commentators, on the significance of its agglomerative ("lumping") quality, which has enabled sex crimes to be lumped together with all manner of unwanted advances, unpleasurable sex, innocent sexploration, and other sexual experiences that are deemed inappropriate but not chargeable as crimes.[24]

That the #MeToo movement is inseparable from the agglomerative Twitter form of its propagation, which enables anyone to claim victimhood under its banner, can be understood as a technologically mediated efflorescence of Catharine MacKinnon's antilegal principle of radical emotional subjectivism: "I call it rape whenever a woman has sex and feels violated."[25] #MeToo reminds us that instead of achieving equality, liberal-carceral feminism's preoccupation with victimhood and the protection of vulnerability proposes instead to universalize the position of subordination historically occupied by women: it betokens a generalized sexual victimology, the associative-agglomerative logic of which mirrors the operation of those bureaucracies of risk that monitor us all. Administering power now actively presumes that at any moment any one of us is "at risk," either of perpetrating sexual misconduct or of becoming a victim of it, so each of us must now be continuously monitored, guided, and, if necessary, corrected or protected by an apparatus of intensive oversight and intervention that is striving to become ever more efficient: ever more vigilant, resourceful, and controlling across all domains of human experience.

The problem is not just that opportunistic or confused people will be led to misconstrue their own experience in this paroxysm of consensus ("feeling-with"), though that certainly is a problem. In socioeconomically individualized times, such opportunities to feel positively and profoundly connected to a larger group are rare; even though the precise nature of the bond and the grounds for this solidarity may sometimes be tenuous and merely affective, as a matter of victimological principle they are never to be questioned in any individual case.[26]

More problematic still is the fact that the agglomerative technics of #MeToo contribute to the erosion of the juridically grounded and rationally accountable form of citizenship that is essential to a functioning democracy. They signal its eclipse by an associative-agglomerative relational logic, a defining characteristic of neoliberalism's political rationality of governance, as this is enacted technically in algorithmic governmentality.[27] #BalanceTonPorc, the equivalent movement in France, also allows users to share their stories of sexual victimization online, though with a greater emphasis on the semipublic shaming of alleged perpetrators. While its website records numerous examples of criminal and morally reprehensible sexual behavior, it also inventories plenty of cases where sex, or expressions of sexual interest, are considered morally reprehensible or are wrongly assumed to be criminal because they happened to be unwanted, or were unpleasurable, or because they were deemed to be otherwise inappropriate—an extremely flexible, inherently agglomerative, and implicitly punitive category if ever there was one: "appropriate" is the new "normal."

The corresponding norm of appropriate sexual relatedness that can be gleaned most readily from the many aberrant self-reports of sexual victimhood that have congregated beneath the banners of these two movements turns out to be a somewhat retouched and updated version of the center of Rubin's "charmed circle": long-term, monogamous, age-appropriate, emotionally intimate attachment.[28] Homosexuality, certain prostheses, pornography (of the softer, erotica type, provided it is not used to "addictive" excess) are no longer quite so stigmatizing, but the taboo on sadomasochism and the insistence on age appropriateness have intensified and been joined by the extremely flexible regulatory concept of addiction, or wariness of "compulsive" sex, which implies, taken together with the ideal of emotional intimacy, that "too much" sex *of any kind* is suspect. In other words, it is occasional or infrequent sex in the context of a long-term secure, amative, intimate, emotionally rich, age-appropriate, and marriage-like relationship that is the new standard.

Attachment Theory: An Administrative Reduction of Psychoanalysis

For the source of this norm of appropriate sex today, we must look to attachment theory, arguably the dominant paradigm of child development in mainstream psychology.[29] It is often assumed that attachment theory is or at least began life as a psychoanalytic theory, in part because John Bowlby, its most renowned exponent, presented it as a corrective development of Freud's work but also because he trained at the Institute of Psycho-Analysis with Joan Rivière and qualified in 1937 as an associate member of the British Psycho-Analytical Society. He went on to train in child analysis with Melanie Klein and became the society's training secretary in the mid-1940s and deputy president in the 1950s. Bowlby also published his *Attachment and Loss* trilogy with Hogarth Press and the Institute of Psycho-Analysis in their joint International Psycho-Analytical Library series.[30] Despite these professional affiliations and circumstantial associations, it would be more accurate to see Bowlby's attachment theory as a powerful reaction against psychoanalysis than as a development of it—a parasitic reduction of psychoanalysis from within its very institutions.

We are not the first to suggest this; the radical incompatibility between Bowlby's theory and psychoanalysis was already noted by prominent psychoanalysts, including Anna Freud, in the early 1960s.[31] It is not simply that Bowlby was first of all a developmental psychologist—before he began his training as a psychoanalyst he had studied developmental psychology at Cambridge, and alongside that training he also studied clinical medicine, qualifying in 1933 and specializing in psychiatry—but more especially that the precedence of developmental psychology in his biography reflects the priority psychology takes over psychoanalysis in his theory.[32]

Bowlby's attachment theory flatly rejects Freud's central assumption that all human subjects are riven by intrapsychic conflict that causes suffering.[33] Instead, Bowlby considered intrapsychic conflict to be the pathological result of observable failings in the caregiving relationship between mother and infant during a formative period from around six months to six years of age, with the first twelve of these months being especially sensitive.[34] For Bowlby the paradigm for pathogenic disturbance in this relationship was "separation":

> a period of separation, and also threats of separation and other forms of rejection, are seen as arousing, in a child or adult, both anxious and angry behaviour. Each is directed towards the attachment figure: anxious attachment is to retain maximum accessibility to the attachment figure; anger is both a reproach at what has happened and a deterrent against its happening again. Thus, love, anxiety, and anger, and sometimes hatred, come to be aroused by one and the same person. As a result painful conflicts are inevitable.[35]

Whereas for Freudian psychoanalysis, to be a battlefield of inner contradictions is the inescapable human condition, for attachment theory the presence of intrapsychic conflict indicates that something has gone wrong during early life: conflict within the psyche can be traced back to a lack of dependable consistency or appropriate affectivity in the mother's responses to her child's needs during this formative period, causing the child to apprehend one and the same person with contradictory emotions. This first attachment relationship is held to be so decisively formative, especially of the capacity to establish successfully trusting relationships with others, that any deficiencies will have grievous consequences later in life.[36]

That Bowlby not only set an extremely exacting standard for appropriate maternal behavior but effectively attributed all of the world's ills to bad mothering has not escaped the notice of feminist critics. For example, Susan Contratto suggests that the infantile determinism of attachment theory and its vision of good mothering have "contributed enormously to women's stress and guilt about doing well by their children."[37] For our part we wish to remark on the resolutely antipsychoanalytic ideals of single-minded coherence and behavioral consistency that inform attachment theory's expectations of good caregivers. We argue that these are fundamentally bureaucratic ideals: if the suffering of intrapsychic conflict is to be avoided, the caregiver must send only unmixed messages to the child, must convey only positive affect (without ambivalence), and must be reliably "available" in these ways whenever needed. Such single-minded attentiveness is possible only if the mother has herself been similarly raised or has benefited from significant therapeutic intervention.[38]

This ideal of single-mindedness as the source and telos of good caregiving is an exact reflection of bureaucratic society, as Herbert Marcuse has characterized it, because of the premium it places on "*one-dimensional thought and behaviour*."[39] By proposing that the suffering of intrapsychic conflict was a pathology caused by deficiencies in the caregiving environment of early childhood, attachment theory amounted to a bureaucratic cancellation of psychoanalysis. The psyche was to be intelligible purely as the predictable product of administrable external reality. This was a utopian fantasy of bureaucratic power: if the world could only be properly administered, then there would be no suffering.

Throughout his career Bowlby was an eager servant of administering power and its fantasies. His early research was overtly criminological: alongside his training in psychoanalysis, he worked in the late 1930s at the Institute for the Scientific Treatment of Delinquency and the London Child Guidance Clinic.[40] His *Forty-Four Juvenile Thieves* recounts his quest at the latter institution for "the springs of delinquent conduct" in the differently defective early childhoods of forty-four young delinquents, all classified by his team according to six character types.[41] This classificatory exercise drew first on the testimony of family members and teachers: "Of the many sources which contribute to this picture undoubtedly the most valuable is the intimate description given of the child by his near relatives. School reports vary in value. An observant mistress will often give the most illuminating reports but others give reports which are useless. Probably the least valuable though none the less essential sources of information were the psychological and psychiatric examinations of the child. The difficulty is that at examinations of this kind children are on their best behaviour and so mask much of their true natures."[42] The methodological premium placed on external observation and examination is striking; to the extent that the children got to speak at all, their words were presumed to be suspect and the "least valuable."

A bureaucratic exercise in classifying from the outside, Bowlby's study is staggeringly pedestrian in its interpretive conclusions, foremost among which is the claim that when children under five are separated from their mothers for long periods they will later express their craving for love by stealing objects as tokens of affection. The study fails to prove empirically that "separation" is the decisive factor in delinquency, for, as Bowlby had to acknowledge, alongside separation there were all manner of other variables for which his study did not control: "poverty, bad housing, lack of recreational facilities and other socio-economic factors . . . will play a large part."[43] Nevertheless, in its methodological commitment to the epistemological primacy of observation, the study offers an early intimation of Bowlby's project to supplant Freud's cure through talking and listening with a surveillant visualism better aligned with administering power.

In an allusion to attachment theory, psychoanalyst André Green underlines the gulf between its surveillant-visualist mode and the different sensory modality of Freud's talking-listening cure:

> If we try to do some research according to scientific methodology, that is, most of the time, with its need of statistical evidence, it is obvious that we shall not be able either to observe, or to label or to classify all that comes under our scrutiny from the couch as parts or expressions of sexuality and destructiveness. We shall only be able to consider the visible part of the iceberg. . . . We prefer to give up the profundity and depth of the unobserved and sometimes unobservable psychic world in order to be proud of our discoveries about the most superficial aspects of psychic life.[44]

Green's suggestion is that the surveillant-visualist sensory modality of attachment theory's proud scientism allows some of the most significant areas of human psychic life to escape attention, in particular sex and destructiveness. He reminds us, in effect, that what Rancière designates as the *partage du sensible* is radically different in each case: "To perceive is to be in connection with external reality. To listen is to be in contact with psychic reality."[45]

Bowlby was quite open about his deliberate decision to opt for observation over listening, yet he appears never to have contemplated the epistemological ramifications of this methodological choice.[46] After World War II he was appointed head of the Children's Department at the Tavistock Clinic, where in 1948 he secured funding for a "separation research unit" to continue his single-minded investigations into the deleterious effects of separation from the mother in early childhood.[47]

The fact that Bowlby was very good at attracting research funding may have had something to do with his aptitude for designing narrowly framed and sensible-sounding empirical studies in a field crowded by intensely speculative, fractious, Continental theorizing, and because he made a point of going over the same ground again and again, the key to specialization then as now.[48] In a 1977 interview he admitted that "one of the reasons that . . . I concentrated on separation was . . . because it was unquestionable—it had either happened or it had not happened."[49] He elaborated in the second volume of his trilogy: "Reasons for concentrating attention on experiences of separation and loss, and of threats of being abandoned, to the exclusion of other events are manifold. In the first place, they are easily defined events that have easily observable effects in the short term and can also, when development continues on a seriously divergent pathway, have easily observable long-term effects. Thus they provide research workers with a valuable point of entry from which to plan projects aimed at casting light on the immensely complex and still deeply shadowed field of personality development and the conditions that determine it."[50] While events of separation may be easy to observe in childhood, what was to have been proven—the *connection* between such events and later expressions of mental illness, or the existence of the connection that would authorize him to speak, as he does here, of the latter as "long-term effects" of the former—is not remotely "observable," easily or otherwise.

Attachment theory's deterministic etiology of mental illness, which attributed it to deficiencies in the early caregiving environment, was never more than an oft-repeated speculative presumption resting precariously on Bowlby's quite arbitrary methodological decision to narrow the scope of his research by focusing on one simply observable facet of the young child's external world. Since there was never any cogent scientific or rational justification for that narrowing, it must be a matter of speculation whether it was undertaken for reasons of convenience, intellectual temperament and experimental design, to facilitate grant capture, or because it reflected back what was most painful in his otherwise privileged biography—distant Edwardian parenting and the separation of boarding school.[51]

Although arbitrary, Bowlby's inaugural decision to focus on observable events of separation fully aligned attachment theory with the surveillant visualism of administering power: the infantile caregiving environment could be inspected and reorganized if found to be deficient. It is not an accident that, on inspection, the failure of this environment to be judged conducive to attachment is the most common ground cited in decisions by British social workers to remove children from their families.[52] Yet most of the population could be persuaded to follow official child-rearing advice simply by the ring of scientific seriousness in claims to "extrapolate forward" from defective childhood caregiving to adult mental illness, combined with the pathos of separation-induced suffering exhibited in Bowlby associate James Robertson's films.[53]

Bowlby's research on separation, coupled with his promulgation of official guidance to mothers, was part of the Tavistock's wider mission to engineer Britain's emerging social welfare democracy in the postwar period. Like other psy-science approaches pioneered under the auspices of this institution, his psychology of child development gained social credibility because of its "perceived or claimed technical capacities to administer persons rationally, in light of a knowledge of what made them tick."[54] In its privileging of a surveillant-visualist sensory modality, attachment theory was neatly aligned with the perspective and imperatives of administering power.

Rather than drawing from psychoanalytic talking-listening, attachment theory derived authority from child observation and from ethology, or the study of animal behavior through observation in laboratory conditions or the natural environment, and from a cognitive model of the mind indebted to cybernetics and perceptual control theory.[55] Coordination of these fields was effected by Bowlby in strikingly administrative parlance: mental functioning is understood in terms of "behavioural systems and their control, of information, negative feedback, and a behavioural form of homeostasis"; language "enables the organisation of behavioural systems in plan hierarchies"; and the individual's emotions or feelings are "a monitoring service regarding his own states, urges, and situations."[56] Attachment figures are classed as "principal" and "subordinate," and even the animal kingdom, as apprehended by ethology, appears to reflect back the naturalness of bureaucratic hierarchies of rank.[57] The good caregiving that produces healthy children is a well-oiled bureaucratic machine, which depends on, "on the one hand, a mother's sensitivity to signals, and her timing of interventions, and, on the other, whether a child experiences that his social initiatives lead to predictable results, and the degree to which his initiatives are in fact successful in establishing a recipro-cal interchange with his mother."[58] The body in attachment theory is the body bureaucratized: the bureaucratized body of a well-attached child is a walking organigram of coordinated systems ready to slot harmoniously into the social organigram of a well-administered social democracy.

Not Too Close: Norms of Appropriate Distance from the "Secure Base"

Bowlby came to characterize optimally attached children in terms borrowed from his collaborator, Mary Salter Ainsworth, a developmental psychologist who joined the Separation

Research Unit in 1950, as "securely attached."[59] In the mid-1960s Ainsworth developed the Strange Situation Procedure, an observational experiment designed to assess the "security" of infants' attachment by separating and reuniting them with their primary caregivers in a laboratory setting and, on the basis of observed reactions, to classify infants according to one of three attachment types: secure, insecure-ambivalent, and insecure-avoidant.[60]

Secure attachment was thought to bring all manner of benefits: "children classified at 15 months as securely attached showed themselves to be more competent socially, more effective in play and more curious, and also more sympathetic to other children's distress, than those earlier classified as insecurely attached."[61] The fact that Bowlby, ever the administrator, presumed that a child could be classified as more "competent" socially or more "effective" at play suggests that no sphere of human experience was safe from appraisal according to norms of functional efficiency. The benefits of secure attachment in early childhood last a lifetime, as this remark by attachment therapist Rhona Fear indicates: "We do not see securely attached individuals in our consulting rooms."[62] In the case of a securely attached child, Ainsworth and Bowlby thought of the mother as the child's "secure base."[63] Good parenting was thus a matter of providing

a secure base from which a child or adolescent can make sorties into the outside world and to which he can return knowing for sure that he will be welcomed when he gets there, nourished physically and emotionally, comforted if distressed, reassured if frightened. In essence this role is one of being available, ready to respond when called upon to encourage and perhaps assist, but to intervene actively only when clearly necessary. In these respects it is a role similar to that of the officer commanding a military base from which an expeditionary force sets out and to which it can retreat, should it meet with a setback. Much of the time the role of the base is a waiting one but it is none the less vital for that. For it is only when the officer commanding the expeditionary force is confident his base is secure that he dare press forward to take risks.[64]

It is not in itself surprising that Bowlby, who lived through two world wars, should have reached for a military analogy. However, it is striking just how intensively and comprehensively the figure of the "secure base" militarizes parenting, dramatizes the social surroundings as an environment full of threat, and along the way reconceives the relationship between parent and child as a gentleman's agreement, a homosocial pact between two senior members of a ruling officer class:

> As a rule a commander-in-chief in charge of front-line forces is also in command of his base. Therefore any threat to his base or to his lines of communication is likely to come only from a single source, the enemy. Let us suppose, by contrast, that the general commanding the front-line forces is not in command of the base, and that another general of equal or superior status is in charge there. In such a situation the general commanding at the front could well have two sources of anxiety, one regarding possible enemy attack and the other regarding possible defection by his colleague at base. Only if there were complete confidence between the two generals could the arrangement be expected to work. A situation of that kind, it is suggested, holds between an individual and his attachment figure.[65]

The security provided by the "secure base" is both material and psychological—a matter of sustaining supply lines and being confident in the possibility of reinforcement or safe retreat when faced with an overwhelming enemy attack or existential "setback." Security of this sort is confidence that allows children to conduct "sorties" without needing to keep checking whether they and the "base commander" are still on the same side. To conceive of parenting in terms of secure attachment to such a base is thus paradoxically to envisage successful parenting as the attainment of a quintessentially middle-class, Edwardian, English norm of appropriate social and bodily *distancing*: intervention is to be envisaged only when "clearly necessary"; the secure base is proximate but *not too close*.

Secure attachment provides the template for later loving relationships in which this norm of distancing informs the presumption, in the dominant model of appropriate relationship, that too much sex is a problem. Bowlby also claimed that the therapist's role was to supply a "secure base" for the patient in a manner that was modeled on the attachment with the parent and that the therapist's duty to "enable his patient to feel some measure of security" was the first task of therapy.[66] By making "security" the first duty of parents, lovers, and therapists alike and the most decisive factor in child development and adult mental health, attachment theory replicates the liberal paradigm of security and renaturalizes it as psychologically necessary for optimal human development. To make all later relationships dependent on this first relationship with the primary caregiver is to perform an infantilizing reduction of nuanced adult social experience into melodramatic oppositions between good and bad caregiving. The more infantilized adult subjects are, the more they need to be governed; the more determining early childhood is in creating individual and social pathology, the more the family environment needs to be shaped by psychotechnical administrators.

If Bowlby's security paradigm was borrowed from Ainsworth, she in turn had adapted it from the "security theory" of William

Blatz, one of her doctoral program supervisors at Toronto.[67] Ainsworth, in her own account of this chain of influence, writes of having "carried over" the concept of the "secure base" into attachment theory and mentions other aspects of Blatz's theory that, thanks to her, were "absorbed into attachment theory."[68] A recent reexamination of this integration concurs that "much of Blatz's work was incorporated" into attachment theory, so much so that perhaps Blatz should be credited as its third founder.[69]

However, these accounts of influence ignore two crucial modifications that Ainsworth and Bowlby made to Blatz's concept of security. For Blatz, an individual's sense of security or lack of it was not a single, stable quality of their psychological identity that exercised a uniform influence across all areas of their life but variable in different areas of their activity: "One person may use a high degree of independent security in his vocation, but be filled with great insecurity in his extra-curricular life. Another may be immaturely dependent in his intimacies but at least assume a high degree of skill and knowledge in his job."[70] The second crucial modification was the conflation of security with safety. Blatz had been adamant: "Safety is the antithesis of independent security. An independently secure person is willing to meet the challenge of living without the protective armour of an agent. He has become his own agent by acquiring self-confidence and self-reliance. He now places his trust in himself. To seek safety is to seek an agent. It is to adopt armour of various kinds, barricades, body-guards, and other similar devices, all of which are vulnerable."[71]

Security, for Blatz, meant self-reliance—the capacity to live without being reliant on external safety measures—but attachment theory turned security into the confidence that such safety measures existed and could be relied on when needed. For attachment theory, the observable existence of safety in the caregiving environment of early childhood would create secure individuals who were equally secure across all of their activities. Bowlby was clear that children's early attachment experience equips them with one particular psychological identity type: whether securely or anxiously attached, or attached in any of the permutations Ainsworth and her followers would later elaborate, children's early attachment experience conferred on them one relatively stable psychological type, by virtue of which they were "a person of this sort."[72] Thus Bowlby and Ainsworth, unlike Blatz, could speak of "an insecure individual," one whose insecurity manifested itself similarly across all areas of their experience. Later attachment-influenced theorists more invested in trauma would classify some children as "secure children," in contrast with the traumatized children with whom they were mainly concerned.[73]

These two tacit modifications were crucial in constructing the "therapeutic authority" of attachment theory, to borrow Peter Miller and Nikolas Rose's term.[74] The conflation of security with safety in the "secure base" meant that the safety of that base was intelligible entirely in terms of administrable external reality, and, if this had been well organized, then the result would be a harmonious individual who could be slotted smoothly into a well-administered society. This vision reflects attachment theory's technocratic hatred of democracy. The simplification of Blatz's more nuanced vision into a single, totalizing category of psychological identity reflected attachment theory's ideal of coherent single-mindedness and helped to establish its "therapeutic authority." After all, if good parenting could not stop children being "insecure" in some areas, then this view would adversely affect the value of research into and advice about it.[75] Regarding attachment theory's later development into traumatology, we argue that these two simplifying modifications to Blatzian "security" have further ramifications.

Returning to "Bygone Times"

Attachment theory's therapeutic authority depended on social acceptance of its scientific credentials. Alongside observational experiments on human infants, Bowlby drew extensively on ethology, the observation of animal behavior within a Darwinian frame.[76] Much of the first volume of Bowlby's *Attachment and Loss* trilogy is concerned with observing attachment behavior in "sub-human species."[77] Attachment behavior is thus presented as part of the "behavioral equipment" that has enabled humankind and other animal species to survive in the face of natural selection.[78]

While this first volume strives to establish impressive scientific credentials for his attachment theory, Bowlby's appeal to evolution inadvertently raises a troubling question about the continuing relevance of attachment, of which he was aware but that he skirts at key junctures: What if attachment behavior had been significant in evolutionary terms but was now a vestigial structure, much as the formation of goose bumps is a vestigial reaction to the threat of attack, no longer of practical use in making us look bigger because we have long since lost our furry pelts? In other words, what if attachment behavior had served its evolutionary purpose but now no longer mattered very much? Bowlby acknowledges that in Darwinian terms the work of natural selection is intelligible only within one particular environment, the *"environment of evolutionary adaptedness."*[79] In the case of human beings, "the primeval natural environment of man, which can probably be defined within reasonable limits, is almost certainly the environment that presented the difficulties and hazards that acted as selective agents during the evolution of the behavioural equipment that still is man's today."[80] Take humankind away from this primeval savannah and it becomes questionable whether any of the "behavioural equipment" forged there—attachment included—continues to serve a useful or significant function.

Although aware of this objection, Bowlby brushed it aside: "All questions as to whether man's present behavioural equipment is adapted to his many present-day environments, especially urban environments, are not strictly relevant to this book, which is concerned only with elemental responses originating in bygone times."[81] Whether the question was "strictly relevant" to that particular book is a moot point, but it most certainly was relevant to the purchase of attachment theory on child rearing in the twentieth century or in other words his theory's wider claim to therapeutic authority. As Bowlby admitted, "When an animal is reared in an environment other than its environment of evolutionary adaptedness . . . the resulting organisation of behaviour may be very different. Sometimes it is bizarre, sometimes inimical to survival. One type of deviant, and often unadapted, behavioural organisation that follows rearing in an atypical environment is illustrated by the literature on unusual animal friendships."[82] There follows a discussion of gay mallards and gay monkeys—though Bowlby does not use this adjective—in which he struggles to attribute the "unusual" character of their "friendships" to their "atypical" surroundings. There is an implication that the unnatural proximity fostered in urban environments may be conducive to the flourishing of nonreproductively focused forms of human sexuality, including homosexuality.

Elsewhere in the volume, in an attempt to illustrate the Darwinian concept of biological function, Bowlby likened a "confirmed homosexual" who achieves "sexual orgasm with a partner of the same sex" to "a radar and predictor-controlled anti-aircraft gun" that shoots down only friendly planes.[83] The second edition of *Attachment and Loss*, in which this extraordinary figure appears, was published in 1982, and what seeps from the narrow frame of its wartime metaphor is not only rank homophobia—gay sex as the misfiring of biological equipment leading to the loss of one's friends—but a wider hatred of sex, in which ejaculate is gunfire and any form of sexual behavior that does not aim at reproduction amounts to a life-threatening malfunction. Those who have opined that attachment theory is, or should be, open to queer desire without bothering to acknowledge the existence of such material will have to try a lot harder.[84]

In his attempt to anchor attachment theory in Darwinian ethology, Bowlby stumbled upon the disarming possibility that attachment behavior might by the mid-twentieth century have outlived its evolutionary usefulness in the human species and be simply a constellation of "elemental responses originating in"—and confined in their relevance to—"bygone times."[85] This never explicitly posed question threatened to undermine the entire edifice of attachment theory. Yet, if contemporary society could be reimagined to resemble the primeval savannah—the human species' environment of evolutionary adaptedness—this question could be dismissed. It just so happened that contemporary society could be reimagined in these neo-Darwinian terms. Bowlby had argued that "the function of attachment behaviour is protection from predators" and that "attachment behaviour is always elicited at high intensity in situations of alarm, which are commonly situations when a predator is either sensed or suspected."[86] If contemporary society were full of dangerous predators, then attachment behavior would be as relevant today as in the primeval savannah.

We do not doubt Bowlby's sincerity when he lamented the extent of child sexual abuse that came to light in the 1970s and 1980s.[87] Yet the conclusion is unavoidable that if modern-day "predators" had not already existed, then attachment theory would have had to invent them, to close a yawning gap between the primeval savannah from which it drew its scientific credentials and the contemporary society in which it made its claim for therapeutic authority. If dangerous predators still lurked, then fear of them could continue to animate a psychology of child development premised on attachment to a secure base in the midst of a hostile world, even in advanced industrial or postindustrial society. If such predators still lurked, then society could be called to order around the ostensibly suprapolitical imperative of child protection: "in no situation are the organisation of the group and role differentiation within it more apparent than when a predator threatens."[88]

As neoliberal reforms of the 1980s in Britain and the United States took away the welfare safety net that had provided working adults with a somewhat secure economic base since World War II, the word *predator* came to acquire, initially in neo-Darwinist crime writing, the sexual and violent sense that would come to be inscribed in the "sexually violent predator" statutes that proliferated in U.S. state legislatures in the 1990s.[89] The next chapter explores the *scientia sexualis* of traumatology, on which these new provisions depended, as a radicalization of attachment theory.

4

Traumatology and Governance

Over the last three decades attachment theory has developed into a victim-centered traumatology exceptionally well attuned to the ideological, social, and economic imperatives of the moment. Whereas John Bowlby's earlier claim to therapeutic authority formed part of the Tavistock's wider project to shape subjects suited to Britain's postwar welfare-state social democracy, today's traumatology flourishes in Britain and the United States within a very different socioeconomic environment: the hypercompetitive individualism of neoliberal capitalism. While the state no longer provides an economic safety net, politicians' promises of more coercive forms of security have become increasingly lavish in a spiraling intensification of the liberal paradigm of security, as citizens demand more and more safety from those who govern them. In the preceding chapter we suggested that the primacy of security in Bowlby's theory made it a consolidating reflection of that paradigm, and we registered the residual militarism in its construction of the "secure base," a reserve of combativeness that has turned out to be extremely well suited to the securitarian mood of the present moment. In this chapter we discuss traumatology as a weaponized form of attachment theory.

The foundational treatise of contemporary traumatology is psychiatrist Judith Herman's *Trauma and Recovery*. First published in 1992, it is firmly grounded in attachment theory:

> The sense of safety in the world, or basic trust, is acquired in earliest life in the relationship with the first caretaker. Originating with life itself, this sense of trust sustains a person throughout the lifecycle. It forms the basis of all systems of relationship and faith. The original experience of care makes it possible for human beings to envisage a world in which they belong, a world hospitable to human life. Basic trust is the foundation of belief in the continuity of life, the order of nature, and the transcendent order of the divine.[1]

The traumatological turn has seen a radicalization of four closely interrelated features of attachment theory that we have suggested were already problematic in their more attenuated forms. First is the commitment to the normative ideal of single-mindedness, against which is contrasted the dissociation of multiple personality, or dissociative identity, disorders held to be caused by trauma: "the genesis of personality fragments, or alters, in situations of massive childhood trauma has been verified in numerous investigations."[2] Second is the related commitment to attachment type as a determining total psychological identity affecting all areas of experience in similarly momentous ways: the effects of trauma are likewise experienced across all areas of experience because "traumatic events produce profound and lasting changes in physiological arousal, emotion, cognition, and memory."[3] Third is the commitment in principle to the lifelong positive effects of good parenting and, conversely, the life-changing negative impact of trauma, paradigmatically childhood sexual abuse: "trauma arrests the course of normal development by its repetitive intrusion into the survivor's life"; "trauma affects every aspect of human functioning."[4] Fourth is the alignment with administrable external reality, expressed in attachment theory's surveillant-visualist sensory modality and its conflation of security with safety. Traumatology frequently progresses from administration into policing as it undertakes a diagnostic evaluation that is suspicious of "the many disguises in which a traumatic disorder may appear."[5]

Traumatology is on the lookout for "perpetrators" behind the "camouflage" of "men of such conventional appearance," and it routinely inspects victims and their present and past environments for traces of abusive behavior, ever vigilant for "the shadow presence of the perpetrator in the relationship between patient and therapist."[6] We focus in this chapter on developing a critical understanding of the therapeutic techniques and theoretical constructions that traumatology has developed from this fourfold radicalization of attachment theory's most problematic dimensions, and we draw attention to some of their less obvious collateral consequences for sex and governance.

Traumatological Therapy in Action

The traumatological turn is entwined with the rise of a liberal-governance-carceral feminism, which privileges victims and their experience. Herman's *Trauma and Recovery* makes this connection explicit, remarking of activist investigators who tackled the sexual politics of rape from the 1970s, "Feminist investigators labored close to their subjects. They repudiated emotional detachment as a measure of the value of scientific investigation and frankly honored their emotional connection with their informants."[7] An intense attachment to the patient is thus expected of the traumatologist, who proceeds in clinical practice to establish the diagnosis: "If the therapist believes the patient is suffering from a traumatic syndrome, she should share this information fully with the patient. Knowledge is power. The traumatized person is often relieved simply to learn the true name of her condition. By ascertaining her diagnosis, she begins the process of mastery. No longer imprisoned in the wordlessness of the trauma, she discovers that there is a language for her experience. She discovers that she is not alone; others have suffered in similar ways."[8]

Susan Rubin Suleiman has cautiously expressed ethical concern about the implications of the clinical approach outlined here.[9] She objects that it implies that therapists will impose their interpretive framework on patients. Herman is indeed very clearly advocating this, in the interests of the patient's recovery, while simultaneously disguising the fact of imposition in a very unusual use of the term "ascertaining" to designate, in a roundabout way, the patient's passivity as recipient of the diagnosis implanted by the therapist. Suleiman also suggests that Herman fails adequately to differentiate between the heuristic-therapeutic value of a trauma diagnosis for patients, as "a conceptual framework" that "provides a reasonable explanation" for their present suffering, and the assumption that the events actually took place as diagnosed, in the absence of any other evidence.[10] Suleiman argues that "if a patient can find relief by constructing a story of childhood trauma that she does not actually recall, or that she recalls only after much 'direct questioning' by the therapist, that is one thing; if the patient then goes on to claim, whether in a court of law or merely in a family circle, that the construction corresponds to historical fact *in the absence of any other evidence*, that is a very different thing."[11]

The allegation that some traumatological therapists deliberately use leading questions to implant "false," or "recovered," memories in suggestible patients has been extensively debated and has been at the forefront of critical resistance to some of the worst excesses of traumatology.[12] It has been established that memories can be altered by suggestion.[13] Here we are concerned less with extreme but probably quite limited examples of deliberate fabrication and focus instead on the more usual scenario of mutual suggestibility, as well as the chilling effects of traumatological techniques and presumptions over a much wider field of ordinary human sexual feeling and experience.

To illustrate this, let us envisage the following scenario, no more or less "fictitious" than the clinical vignettes that Herman confects for the purpose of her own demonstration.[14] All human beings, as they grow up, inevitably encounter some degree of benign sexual oddity or awkwardness in themselves and other people, even if only in their own desire. If they are prone to worry and are suffering, in this or other ways, they may consult a therapist. Indeed, if they are already worrying about a past encounter with ordinary sexual oddity in another person, they may seek out a therapist who advertises an expertise in sexual traumatology. The current prevalence of traumatology in the media makes it all the more likely that such encounters will become points of neurotic fixation. When they enter therapy, they may be wondering whether or not they should be worried about that earlier experience and whether it can explain their present suffering. They may encounter a clinician who already has a strong theoretical and political commitment to the diagnostic "naming" of trauma, even in situations where the patient has never construed their experience as traumatic or suspected that past trauma may be the root of their present suffering; they may encounter a clinician who is theoretically and politically inclined to validate the very worst fears of the neurotic patient who has already entertained this as one possibility alongside myriad other anxieties. They may face a clinician who holds to the dubious claims of the radicalized form of attachment theory we have outlined, according to which a traumatic event will be thought to have had a decisive impact across all areas of their subsequent life and experience, an impact that only more therapy can assuage. They may face a clinician who, having "named" the trauma for the patient, will then "explain" the "personality deformations" that result from that trauma.[15]

To "explain" in this way cannot be considered a straight-forward act of communicating information, since it occurs within the intensely transferential dynamic of the therapeutic relationship and implies definite expectations about the patient's feelings and experiences. Notwithstanding Suleiman's concern about traumatologists imposing their understanding on patients unidirectionally, the more likely danger is that a climate of mutual suggestibility will be established, one in which patients predispose themselves to accept the traumatological reconstruction that the therapist is predisposed to offer, in the manner indicated by Mikkel Borch-Jacobsen: "Good hypnotists have always known that initially suggestibility is always autosuggestion or, more precisely, a consensual suggestion, *negotiated* with the hypnotist. In fact, it starts the very instant the patient decides to visit the 'medicine man,' turning himself over to this man (or his theory), in order to make his ills disappear."[16] Traumatologists will work this extremely fertile ground of "consensual suggestion" to co-construct the traumatic case history with patients and co-curate their victimized identity, including by advising them how they should expect to feel as therapy advances.

In this hypothetical scenario, in which highly suggestible patients with worries about past experience of benign sexual inappropriateness and case histories of suffering in the present eagerly collaborate with therapists to recode their experience as abuse and leave therapy with a fully fledged survivor-victim identity, they may well feel like very satisfied customers since all of their present suffering is ostensibly now intelligible. However, this "therapy" will not necessarily have helped them because, while it may impel them to reorganize aspects of their external environment, it will not bring long-term resolution of neurotic symptoms that were not, in fact, caused by the co-constructed traumatic history. If you think this scenario too implausible a fiction, then you underestimate the way in which people take their cues about what to worry about from the news media, which for thirty years has deluged us with reports of lives wrecked by abuse. Many of these stories are true of course, and the suffering involved can be terrible, yet their truth and intensity make them ideal points of fixation for neurotic anxiety in others, who may not even seek out therapy but who nevertheless overidentify and embark on their own recoding of benign sexual inappropriateness as abuse, which is misinterpretation that can engender untold new suffering.

Not all patients will be as receptive or suggestible as our hypothetical neurotics, particularly in cases where a patient has come to therapy without any specific worries about past sexual experience. In such cases, in Herman's experience, "the patient's symptoms simultaneously call attention to the existence of an unspeakable secret and deflect attention from that secret. The first apprehension that there may be a traumatic history often comes from the therapist's countertransference reactions. The therapist experiences the inner confusion of the abused child in relation to the patient's symptoms. . . . Therapists often report uncanny, grotesque, or bizarre imagery, dreams, or fantasies while working with such patients. They may themselves have unaccustomed dissociative experiences, including not only numbing and perceptual distortions but also depersonalization, derealization, and passive influence experiences."[17] If a therapist feels confused or has strange dreams, then this, Herman suggests, "may" be a "first apprehension" of a hidden traumatic history. It may be, but it may not be.

For clinicians seeing several patients in one day, there are presumably practical difficulties in tying any "grotesque" or "bizarre" dreams to one particular patient. Let us suppose, however, for the sake of argument that the traumatologist can correctly identify the patient in relation to whom the bizarre dream has its meaning. In her manual of traumatology Herman is *suggesting* to clinicians—we use the emphasized term advisedly—that when therapists have strange dreams or experience "inner confusion," these "may" be "countertransferential reactions" that indicate the patient has a hidden history of abuse. They may be, but they may not be: they could just as well be the expression of ordinary passing confusion or a disturbed night's sleep. However, Herman is suggesting that whenever therapists have such a feeling in their countertransferential waters, a feeling potentially as inchoate as "inner confusion," they should try to ascertain whether their patient has a hidden traumatic history. It is clear that the therapist will begin this investigative-diagnostic process predisposed, by the force of Herman's own suggestions, to the idea that such a history really exists. In the case of a patient who was sexually abused, this will likely lead to the excavation of that history, but in the case of a patient who was not sexually abused, it will begin the process of identifying past exposure to benign sexual inappropriateness and recoding it as abuse.

As they begin to look for traumatic history, therapists who might otherwise be inclined to exercise ordinary skepticism are cautioned by Herman—again, suggestively—that this "may" be their inadvertent identifying with the perpetrator: "Identification with the perpetrator may take many forms. The therapist may find herself becoming highly skeptical of the patient's story, or she may begin to minimize or rationalize the abuse."[18] A community of no doubt well-meaning traumatological therapists is thus suggestively preconditioned by Herman and other leading specialists to begin looking for evidence of abuse on the flimsiest of grounds, to construct it where it may be lacking, from any available examples of benign sexual inappropriateness, and to doubt any spontaneous reactions they may have that contextualize or rationalize ("minimize") that material.

The viciously efficient circularity thus inscribed in the clinical technique of contemporary traumatology has produced some of its most lurid effects in the case of "satanic ritual abuse." Social anthropologist Jean La Fontaine led a three-year UK Department of Health inquiry into eighty-four cases of "satanic ritual abuse" investigated by police and social workers between 1988 and 1991. In her 1994 report and subsequent monograph, La Fontaine acknowledged that in many of these cases evidence of severe sexual and physical abuse had been found, yet she identified the satanic element as a myth co-constructed by vulnerable children in foster care and a community of therapists militantly committed to believing victims: "Among many who work in this field, believing the victim has become an unquestioned dogma that disregards any need for corroborative evidence."[19]

From her examination of records of interviews with alleged victims, La Fontaine concluded that therapists and social workers had exposed the children to many hours of highly suggestive questioning before they made their "disclosures": "Failure to find out from the child what happened is taken as evidence of something extremely serious, requiring interviews to induce the first stage of healing: disclosure. The interval between taking children into care and their 'disclosures' of satanic abuse may be filled with a long series of 'therapeutic interviews.' Sometimes as many as eighty hours of interviews are required to obtain a 'disclosure' that may be taken as evidence of satanic abuse."[20] Just as Herman warned traumatologists to be suspicious of the "many disguises" in which a traumatic disorder may appear, so silence or outright denial was interpreted by therapists and interviewers as evidence for the existence of satanic ritual abuse:

Failure to disclose, denials or silence are often interpreted by believers as evidence of the deep trauma and/or intimidation the child has suffered. It might be believed that children had words implanted into their subconscious that, when spoken, would release a memory of what would happen if they made a disclosure and prevent them answering questions. These are referred to as trigger words. . . . Refusal to confirm what was suspected or to answer questions at all was in some cases considered evidence of the operation of trigger words and hence of satanic abuse. Satanic abuse thus provides an explanation for the failure to establish what happened.[21]

When they "disclosed," the children invariably did so to foster parents, many of whom expected additional payments for looking after such traumatized children.[22] La Fontaine highlighted the role that conferences of therapists had played in spreading the idea that "a new form of abuse had been discovered," along with the mingled feelings of prestige and nervousness felt by adults and social workers about being "in the vanguard of such discoveries."[23]

Prominent traumatologists have proven curiously impervious to the damning conclusions of La Fontaine's report. One of the most vocal crusaders against "satanic ritual abuse," Valerie Sinason, countered with the publication of her own coauthored "study" of the phenomenon, which concluded with the extraordinary recommendation that "personnel involved in the investigation, as in the new rape suites and child protection units, need to offer a basic stance of belief in the patient's narrative until proven otherwise."[24]

Sinason is closely associated with the Centre for Attachment-Based Psychoanalytic Psychotherapy, a London traumatology clinic accredited by the UK Council for Psychotherapy (UKCP) and also known as the Bowlby Centre; she addressed their 2006 annual conference and keynoted a 2009 conference on "ritual abuse and mind control" organized under the auspices of the center, the proceedings of which were edited by three individuals having long-standing associations with the center, including the current editor of its journal.[25]

Despite having published a book in 1994 on treating "survivors" of "satanic abuse," Sinason in 2009 was initially cagey about the "satanic" element, remarking simply that "in the late 1980s and early 1990s, almost everyone we saw said he or she was a survivor of Satanist abuse" but that "later referrals included Luciferians, those from Paganism, Wicca, Voodoo, Black Witchcraft, Black Dianetics, Gnostic Luciferianism, Illuminati, Military Mind Control, MK Ultra, and Bluebird."[26] We surmise that organizers of the 2009 conference made a tactical decision to emphasize the "ritual" element because the "satanic" dimension had been so resoundingly discredited by La Fontaine. However, contributors clearly had some difficulty sticking to this plan. Sinason effectively admitted to precisely the epistemological failing that La Fontaine had identified; indeed, she upheld it as an enduring principle of her own clinical practice: "After further years of work, survivors were able to let us know that there were some areas of terror where, *if we named the unnameable*, they would be free to express more."[27]

Perhaps the most extraordinary part of this extraordinarily revealing conference publication is a forty-eight-page appendix following Sinason's text and titled "Calendar Abuse—The Significance of Ritual Dates." This "calendar," compiled from a ragbag of sources, including the testimony of "survivors," is introduced by Sinason in the following terms: "When children and adults made their brave way to speaking of abuse within religious or cult systems in the 1980s, they showed, through their verbal and non-verbal responses, that certain dates held enormous terror for them."[28] Entries include religious festivals and public holidays; an example is "April . . . 20–Queen's Day (Netherlands)," one of a number of factually erroneous listings, since Queen's Day was celebrated on April 30 until the abdication of Queen Beatrix in 2013.[29]

These notionally factual entries sit alongside the following type of entry, ostensibly for the day before, April 19: "This is the first day of the thirteen-day Satanic ritual relating to fire, the fire god, Baal, or Molech/Nimrod (the Sun God), also known as the Roman god, Saturn (Satan/Devil). This day is a major human sacrifice day, demanding fire sacrifice with an emphasis on children. This day is one of the most important sacrifice days in Satanist abuse groups."[30] The entry for May 1 reads, "May Day. Beltane Fire Festival. Major Celtic festival. This is the Greatest Sabbat, and is marked by fertility rites in open fields. Seminal fluid is mixed with dirt and insects and inserted into the vagina of a virgin. If conception occurs, the children are children of Tiamet and Dur (Indur)."[31] In between entries for D-Day and Father's Day, under June 21 we find this: "Summer Solstice. Can be marked by torture, rape, and sacrifice of traitors, sacrifice and consumption of an infant."[32] This incredible "calendar" is said by Sinason to be "an aid to looking at triggers linked to belief systems."[33]

Perhaps since the conference it has served as such an "aid" to traumatologists in suggesting to patients why they may be feeling bad. The "calendar" and the publication in which it appears are eloquent about this particular lunatic fringe of traumatology: not only are the "satanic" claims strongly reasserted in the calendar as though they were facts, but its blending of utterly outlandish material from "survivors" with quite ordinary dates and festivals is an object lesson in propagandistic misinformation. It serves a function similar to the "lists of 'indicators'" of satanic ritual abuse circulated by therapists and denounced in the preceding decade by La Fontaine for their role in spreading that particular abuse panic.[34]

Other contributions to the same Bowlby Centre volume exhibit similarly troubling propensities. One therapist, who worked as a training analyst at the center, reports in her case history of "Jodi" that "when Jodi had reached puberty, *as with all female ritual abuse survivors*, she was forced to kill her baby, whose birth had been prematurely induced by the cult doctor."[35] As "Jodi" drew pictures of "the cult which abused her," her therapist was overwhelmed: "During this period, in my notes I wrote, 'nausea, blood, semen, vomit, sweat: *the room reeks of them*. Like it's pouring down the walls.'"[36] This appears to be a therapist admitting to having experienced an overwhelming olfactory hallucination in her own consulting room. Another contributor, Ellen Lacter, asserts, "Some of the strongest corroborative evidence for mind control is a 2007 internet survey in which 1471 people from at least forty countries responded as survivors to *the Extreme Abuse Survey* (EAS) (Becker, Karriker, Overkamp, & Rutz, 2007). . . . 1: Torture to induce the formation of receptive/programmable dissociated self-states. Of 1012 EAS respondents who replied to the item: 'My perpetrator(s) deliberately created/programmed dissociative states of mind (such as alters, personalities, ego-states) in me,' 640 (63%) said 'Yes.'"[37] That responses to this pseudoscientific survey do not constitute remotely credible "evidence" for the existence of "mind control" should be obvious. Lacter subsequently introduces the following testimony of one Carol Rutz as though it were trustworthy: "Rutz (2003) explains that her programming was eventually accomplished with hypnosis alone: All the programming that was done to me by the CIA *and Illuminati* was trauma-based using things like electroshock, sensory deprivation, and drugs."[38]

Lacter offers the following guidance to therapists on how to "reset" the "triggers" programmed into "survivors" by "cults": "Programme reset codes can be changed to impossible stimuli, for example, a one-inch tall baby giraffe with peppermint breath whistling Dixie."[39] Orit Badouk Epstein, editor of the Bowlby Centre's journal, remarks in her case history of work with an alleged victim of ritual abuse—a case history that reads, much like the case history by Rachel Wingfield Schwartz, as one long *folie à deux*—that "Christmas is one of the hardest times for our survivors. It is time [*sic*] *when human sacrifice takes place* and when our clients were most terrorized and abused."[40] The center that hosted this conference and published this arrant nonsense is still operating today, in London; it enjoys UKCP accreditation and makes around £250,000 annually by training therapists and social workers, which is to say that it is financed to a large extent by British taxpayers.

The excesses of this lunatic fringe would be comical were it not for the fact that the desperate people who feature in these case histories (and presumably hundreds of others that are not reported) were real people who were clearly suffering and deserved far better therapy than they got. One example is Carole Myers, whose suicide has been persuasively attributed by investigative journalist Will Storr to Sinason's catastrophic failure of clinical technique in validating persecutory delusions that she had suffered satanic ritual abuse at the hands of her parents.[41] However, the excesses of this lunatic fringe cannot be neatly severed from mainstream traumatology's general approach. Many of the therapists refer explicitly to Herman, and the toxic clinical dynamic displayed in the construction of these (satanic) ritual abuse cases can be shown to stem directly from inherent limitations in the clinical technique and professional ethic championed by Herman as the precious insight of an activist feminism committed to always believing the victim. The climate of suggestibility cultivated in Herman's traumatology and her reliance on suggestion in promoting her approach are of a piece with the activities of this lunatic fringe. After all, did Herman not warn that "trauma is contagious" and that the therapist would at times be "overwhelmed"?[42] This recalls the early modern witch hunts in which the community suggested itself into "a form of mass hysteria."[43]

The narrow point about traumatology we have illustrated with the hypothetical scenario of the neurotic patient is that traumatology functions as a highly effective machine for recoding ordinary, benign sexual oddity or inappropriateness as sexual abuse. Neurotic people often consult experts to tell them whether or not they should worry about something in the first place. It is very doubtful whether anyone, least of all the "victim" in our scenario, is helped by encountering a clinician who validates one of their worst fears by telling them they have indeed been sexually abused, that their present suffering is intelligible primarily in terms of that traumatic event, and that some other person is to blame for everything. The wider point is that the propensity of traumatology to recode benign sexual inappropriateness as abuse has intensely normalizing consequences far beyond those clinical encounters. If inappropriateness, or benign sexual oddity, can retrospectively be recoded as abuse, then this has a powerfully dissuasive impact on sex in general. It inclines us all to maintain extreme vigilance in sexual matters, to eschew sexual situations as potentially dangerous, and even to deny any interest in sex outside the monogamous marriage-like, intimate but only occasionally sexual relationship of secure attachment. Traumatology teaches hatred of sex.

Curating Victim Identity

Although it would be an error to reduce traumatology to its socioeconomic context, some of its most problematic features cannot be adequately understood without careful reference to that neoliberal moment. We develop such a contextualization in this section. We have referred to "traumatology," even though the term is not in common use, because Herman and her followers consider the extraordinary nature of the experiences they attend to means that their theoretical constructions and therapeutic practices surpass those of ordinary therapy: "In general, the diagnostic categories of the existing psychiatric canon are simply not designed for survivors of extreme situations and do not fit them well. The persistent anxiety, phobias, and panic of survivors are not the same as ordinary anxiety disorders. The somatic symptoms of survivors are not the same as ordinary psychosomatic disorders. Their depression is not the same as ordinary depression. And the degradation of their identity and relational life is not the same as ordinary personality disorder."[44]

Traumatology presents itself as a radical development of existing psy-science so as to take account of hitherto unrecognized (or underrecognized) horrors, and also as a body of knowledge that trumps and subsumes the claims of existing practice and theory. Traumatology suggests that trauma-induced suffering is more severe and more deserving of attention than other forms of mental and physical suffering. It makes a totalizing or agglomerating claim over existing forms of therapy and presents itself as an expressly political project for the moralizing transformation of society around the victim and their experience, one that begins in the traumatological clinic.[45]

This claim to deploy an optimized form of superior theoretical insight and therapeutic practice specially adapted to the particular needs of a particular set of patients is especially powerful in a competitive marketplace for therapy. Indeed, it is extremely well attuned to the neoliberal moment's privileging of an optimally satisfying customer "experience" of therapy. If traumatology's methods and categories are more powerful than other forms of therapy and if traumatic experience is more serious—more "special"—than other forms of suffering, then that is clearly also a strong sales pitch.

The marketplace for therapy is increasingly competitive, especially in the United States, because since the 1960s the rate of growth in the number of mental health professionals has significantly outstripped growth rates of the general population.[46] Philip Jenkins notes of that national context that "the child abuse issue validated and encouraged the growing prestige of the therapeutic professions: from 1970 to 1993, the ranks of the American Psychological Association more than doubled, from 30,839 to 75,000 members, and those of the American Psychiatric Association swelled from 18,407 to 38,000 members. By the late 1980s, more than 250,000 psychologists were employed in various capacities in the United States."[47] It may be said that such an increase should be welcomed as a humane response to the discovery of hitherto unrecognized abuse during these years. Certainly there is a great deal more sexual abuse of children in the world than was imagined in 1950. Nevertheless, if traumatology's clinical technique and methodological commitments predispose it to recode ordinary benign sexual inappropriateness as abuse, and if the professional standing of traumatological experts grows in step with public perception of the extent of abuse, then this is remarkably propitious because it constitutes a self-supporting set of circumstances for rapid business growth. While it would be an error of analysis and a failure of empathy to reduce the traumatological clinic to the provision of a service to a customer, it also would be an analytical error to ignore that dimension.

Other businesses would do almost anything to secure from their customers the kind of staunch and vocal loyalty that most "survivors" lavish on their traumatological therapists. Satisfied customers of the traumatological clinic are usually very satisfied indeed and will readily credit their therapist. One of Herman's patients explains why: "Good therapists were those who really validated my experience."[48] Viewed from this angle, the commitment to always believing the victim appears not only as an ethical or methodological principle but also as the basis of an extremely strong bond with the supplier of a service; always believing the victim is also a commercial imperative. Another satisfied customer quoted by Herman describes the good therapist in these terms: "It's like being a good coach."[49] Herman elaborates by citing the following "metaphor" developed by her traumatologist colleague Terence Keane: "I felt like a coach when I started out. That's because I played basketball, and I just felt it: I was the coach and this was a game, and this is how you play the game, and this is the way to go, and the object is to win. I don't say that to patients, but that's how it feels to me."[50]

To construe winning as the object of this particular truth-game—and the good traumatologist as a "coach" who "validates" the "experience" of the paying customer—meshes extremely well with the fiercely competitive individualism of the neoliberal moment. William Davies has shown how neoliberalism requires "new breeds of expert coach, regulator, risk manager, strategist, guru" who "construct and help navigate a world of constant, overlapping competitions."[51] It is within this wider socioeconomic paradigm that traumatologists "coach" their patients, providing a service that promises to transmute the base metal of abuse or other suffering into the gold of victimized identity. In countries such as the United States and Britain, which have liquidated governments' capacity to provide citizens with the security of an economic safety net, Roger Lancaster states, only a touch hyperbolically, that "victims—and *only* victims—might be entitled to support, services, and assistance, at a time when 'welfare' was being made a dirty word. All that was required was the naming of a victimizer."[52]

There is more to this than just the establishing of legal claims to scarce resources. Traumatologists offer their therapeutic services and the victimized, "survivor" identity they co-curate as a powerful component in what Ulrich Bröckling has characterized, based on Foucault's comments, as the obligatory entrepreneurship of the neoliberal self.[53] Drawing on Ian Hacking's conceptualization of "making up" people (which is not equivalent to mere fabrication), Ruth Leys argues in her incisive study of trauma that "PTSD is a way of 'making up' a certain type of person that individuals can conceive themselves as being and on the basis of which they can become eligible for insurance-reimbursed therapy, or compensation, or can plead diminished responsibility in courts of law."[54]

Leys is careful not to reduce traumatology and its diagnostic constructions to the economic and social transactions that surround and traverse them, yet neither does she ignore them. She explains that current scientific understanding of trauma was shaped in significant ways by psychoanalyst William Niederland's pioneering work, which had a significant legal-economic dimension, first in Germany with Holocaust survivors and later in the United States with Vietnam veterans. Leys argues that because of German courts' initially unsympathetic responses to Holocaust survivors, doctors helping victims bring claims for compensation had "to insist on the centrality of the horrors of the camps to their patients' subsequent problems"; she asserts there was a similar imperative for Vietnam veterans seeking financial redress from the U.S. Veterans Administration and other government bureaucracies.[55]

In both cases Leys suggests that this situation significantly influenced the scientific construction of trauma, PTSD, and related concepts: trauma-based claims for compensation in post–Nazi Germany or post–Vietnam War America were initially made in a climate of legal skepticism and shared the "same need to tie pathology directly to the occasioning event by conceptualizing symptoms as if they were the direct, if delayed, reaction to a trauma on the model of an inflammatory response to a foreign body."[56] This history has shaped the dominant model of trauma's effects that is shared by poststructuralist "trauma theorists" and leading traumatological psychiatrists alike, such as Judith Herman and Bessel van der Kolk—a model according to which the intensity of the traumatic event is thought to overwhelm the brain's capacity for normal cognition and memory, inscribing itself directly on the victim's mental apparatus in a "*literal* registration of the traumatic event that, dissociated from normal mental processes of cognition, cannot be known or represented but returns belatedly in the form of 'flashbacks,' traumatic nightmares, and other repetitive phenomena."[57]

Although "dismayed by the low quality of Van der Kolk's scientific work" generally and struck by the "flimsiness of the evidence" in one paper on PTSD dreams especially, Leys registers the authority that other members of the traumatological community accord van der Kolk's research on the neurobiology of trauma.[58] The neurobiological account of traumatic memory with which he is associated draws on laboratory research into animal responses to "inescapable shock"—typically experiments on rats that have electrodes implanted in their heads and are confined in heated cages—to argue that traumatic stress causes the release of high levels of the hormone and neurotransmitter norepinephrine, or noradrenaline, which modifies the brain in ways that cause the later intrusion of nightmares and other symptoms.[59] The release of large amounts of noradrenaline depletes reserves and creates a vicious cycle in which a feeling of helplessness is produced, which depletes reserves further.[60] Leys adds,

> A related assumption connects the hyperreactivity of PTSD patients, as manifested in startle responses, sleep difficulties, anxiety, and other symptoms, to phases in the production of endogenous opiates, or endorphins, such that the anxiety

produced by trauma releases endorphins, which produces a sense of relief, which is followed by endorphin depletion, which induces hyperreactivity and anxiety, with the result that the cycle begins again. The relief associated with endorphins is thought to make the victim of trauma "addicted" to the trauma, as when the victim of sexual abuse repeatedly seeks out similar abusive situations.[61]

This neurobiological account of the way trauma writes itself directly on the survivor's brain is tacitly informed, Leys argues, by the climate of legal skepticism in which the first claims for compensation by survivors were brought, in Germany and the United States. Our account of the radicalization by traumatology of some of attachment theory's most problematic assumptions argues that the theoretical, therapeutic, and ethical deficiencies of traumatology stem also from the model of the healthy mind it takes from attachment theory and against which it constructs its symptomatology of trauma. The idea that good parenting creates a secure, single-minded, and determining psychological identity is the implicit but highly dubious standard, or baseline, against which the dysfunction of traumatized subjects is conceived, whether neurobiologically or otherwise.

Van der Kolk's work holds considerable prestige among traumatological therapists. Yet, even if his neurobiological model of trauma were accurate (which seems unlikely), then it would not account for why some patients seem far more susceptible to being traumatized than others, and neither would it justify treating the aftereffects of trauma with long years of talking therapy, rather than with short courses of pharmacological remedies combined with cognitive-behavioral "rewiring." Nor does it stand without the neurobiology of addiction and an implicitly moralizing presumption that addictive neurocircuitry is inferior or damaging. Nor is it cognizant of the climate of coordinated suggestibility that pervades contemporary traumatology and the aforementioned problem of mimetic-neurotic self-traumatization—the production of self-wounding subjects, which is an unexpected but pervasive collateral consequence of the prominence of traumatology in contemporary culture. A model of trauma based on the direct inscription of an external event on the individual brain cannot adequately account for all of these complex interpersonal ramifications.

It is important to acknowledge that traumatology's rise to prominence makes it an exceptional business success story in neoliberal times. The loyalty of satisfied customers to their therapists is something that other businesses would find enviable, as is the remarkable rate of growth in the therapy enterprise. Traumatology's proximity to the juridical, combined with its very low, often nonexistent requirement for corroborating evidence, also makes it an attractive option for frauds and fakers. For such subjects, the traumatological clinic promises quick relief from the excessive burden of individualized responsibility that we are all made to bear under neoliberalism for our failures and successes.

As a way of "making up" people, in Hacking's sense, the co-curation of victimized identity by traumatologists may also help real victims of abuse, yet such astonishing rates of business growth have been achieved only by tacitly but very considerably widening the scope of the category of "abuse" and doing so with complete indifference to the collateral consequences. As we prepare to exit the traumatologist's clinic, we wish to underline three related senses in which their technique is totalizing, or agglomerating: (1) the diagnosis of a traumatic history encompasses every aspect of a subject's life and the entire range of symptoms; (2) traumatology subsumes in agglomerating fashion and surpasses every other kind of therapy, just as traumatic suffering is more serious and significant than other forms of suffering; and (3) the traumatological clinic attaches the validating therapist to the grateful patient in a dyad of sustenance and mutual suggestibility that in turn binds both to an agglomerated, though largely notional, global community of victims.

The Proper Processes

Since the cultural effects of traumatology resonate far beyond the clinic, in this concluding section we explore the ways in which they serve governance. Traumatology is not the first theoretico-technical ensemble to make use of human self-doubt in sexual matters in ways that serve governing power. Traumatology can be understood as continuous with earlier techniques through which pastoral power fashioned governable subjects by exploiting the human propensity to hate sex. However, traumatology's effects must also be understood in terms of the particular type of governing power that has flourished under neoliberal capitalism: "governance." Governance can be understood as the colonization of every area of social reality by self-optimizing techniques of administration derived from business management; governance betokens the overwhelming of democratic politics and the juridically accountable individual subject by the agglomerating techniques of algorithmic governmentality, while also pitting individuals against one another in a highly competitive world reengineered as a series of interlocking competitions.

Traumatology divides the world into abuser-predators and survivor-victims, simplifying social reality into both the one-dimensional form favored by administering power and the melodramatic play of opposites, ever beloved of the news media. The foundational impropriety of sex is covered over, as traumatological dogma demands of us all a constant vigilance over our thoughts, feelings, and actions—a constant neurotic self-interrogation about whether we may inadvertently have been abusive or coercive, rather than merely inappropriately persuasive. It also encourages us to view other people with similar suspicion and to laud the public exhibition of such soul-searching, as in penitential rituals of the early and medieval Church.

Nevertheless, neoliberal governance describes a secular and global form of power that thrives independently of any particular national, religious, or cultural tradition. Traumatology's attempt to recall the world to order around the ostensibly suprapolitical imperative to protect the vulnerable from predators readily serves the global, secular, universalist ambitions of governance. When traumatology encounters a social institution—a religious organization or a university, for example—it tends to insist that new administrative protocols, scripts, or "processes" be devised to better serve victims in future. Traumatology thus seeks to script in advance the thoughts and interactions of employees, as well as radically curb their room to exercise discretion, thus acting as a powerful justification for the further proletarian-ization of middle-class professional labor. Teachers, priests, politicians, doctors, social workers, and other professionals thus cannot be trusted because they have "failed" victims in the past. As a result, they must now be told how to think and behave, and if they can be told how to think about this, then they can be told how to think about anything.

For governance, traumatology models and intensifies the subject's extreme susceptibility to the suggestions of power: if only the governed could, in all their activities, be as open to accepting direction as the client is to the constructions of their therapist. If only the hateable messiness of democracy and sex could be replaced by the climate of suggestibility between trau-matological therapists and their clients, where suggestions bring order and orders are issued by suggestion. If only the governed could be securely attached to their rulers. If only all suffering could be explained as confidently as traumatology does: for those who are suffering but are unsure why, traumatology constructs and curates an agglomerating victimized identity in relation to which all of their manifold misfortune becomes intelligible.

Traumatology teaches hatred of democracy by suggesting that the human capacity to abuse others legitimates the proliferation of bureaucracies of risk to monitor all of us and the spread of protocols of obedience so that we know to handle the victimized appropriately. Traumatology teaches hatred of sex by wielding—indeed, proliferating—the extreme category of "abuse." By doing so, it not only targets abuse but disciplines the much wider field of benign sexual inappropriateness and sex in general in a way that seeks to secure appropriate sexual behavior—in other words, occasional or infrequent sex in the context of a long-term, secure, amative, intimate, emotionally rich, age-appropriate, and marriage-like relationship.

Afterword

The Hatred of Sex in Hatred of Democracy

We wrote *Hatred of Sex* during the Trump administration. Here we reflect on our book's claims in light of the cataclysm that pushed his administration over the cliff, namely, the storming of the U.S. Capitol on January 6, 2021, an event that expressed hatred of democracy in particularly violent fashion. Having stressed the significance of "disorder" in Rancière's account of democracy, we begin by noting that the Capitol riot does not exemplify the disorder he identifies with democracy in its original form. Rancière gestures toward this distinction when he describes the events of January 6 as an "unleashing of the purest irrationality at the heart of the electoral process, in the country best set up to manage alternation in a representative system."[1]

The peaceful transfer of power from one democratically elected government to the next is a hallmark of constitutional democracies and a cherished political norm in the United States. Disrupting that transfer of power, whether through violent insurrection or the rhetoric of delegitimation, betokens not democracy's disordering but its subversion in favor of dictatorship. And yet we still need to account for the way in which the insurrectionists understood themselves as *saving* democracy—saving it from powerful elites who had abused not only the electoral process ("Stop the steal!") but also hordes of sexually innocent children along the way.

Conspiracy theories have a long history in the U.S. political system, as Richard Hofstadter demonstrated more than fifty years ago.[2] However, the QAnon conspiracy that captured the imagination of so many and helped to motivate the Capitol insurrection is marked by several distinct features: the ease with which it propagated algorithmically online, exploiting new information technologies; the degree to which it counterintuitively presented social media users with enigmas to be solved rather than ready-made explanations; and above all its investment in pedophilic fantasies of child abuse for which, we suggest, the ground was laid by traumatology. All those rioters emblazoned with the letter Q were preoccupied neither with queers nor with the same-sex issues that triggered previous culture wars but with the imaginary spectacle of prominent older women, such as Hillary Clinton and Nancy Pelosi, trafficking children for sex rituals. If the storming of the Capitol aimed to redress Trump's election defeat, it nevertheless also involved saving children from sexual predation, with the passions inflamed by lurid tales of abuse stoking the insurrectionists' wild-eyed determination to restore their loser leader. The assault on the Capitol thus furnishes an opportunity for grasping connections between hatred of democracy and hatred of sex.

Hatred of sex tends to be justified by the belief that sex is uniquely harmful. Our view on this matter is encapsulated by the psychoanalyst André Green when he writes that "there is no better way to castrate Eros than to make him harmless."[3] Sex is rendered harmless under neoliberalism by annexing it to identity, with the excess coded as always potentially injurious to others and specifically sexual pleasure seen as extracted at others' expense. Identity is one of the most powerful prophylactics through which sex is made safe. We have argued, to the contrary, that sex is not harmless: it violates propriety and the appropriate, just as its excessive pleasures threaten the coherence of human egos and thereby challenge identity. Sexual pleasure is both longed for and hated because it disrupts, disorders, renders deplorable, and shatters our dignity. But, if sex is not harmless, does it necessarily follow that liberal-governance-carceral feminists, along with traumatologists in the psy-sciences, are right to regard all sex as potentially abusive? Does the manner in which sex is *not* harmless justify the proliferating sex bureaucracies in their constant vigilance for actionable instances of sexual harm? Here we join scholars such as Joseph Fischel and Avgi Saketopoulou in an effort to rethink the ostensibly self-evident category of sexual harm by elaborating further our concept of "benign sexual inappropriateness."[4]

In *Hatred of Sex* we have returned to Freud (in this case via Jean Laplanche) to stress how sexual pleasure's propensity for unbinding remains incommensurate with the human ego as a quintessentially bound form. Resistance to the theoretical radicalism of Freud's insights into human sexuality is as old as psychoanalysis itself—resistance not just from skeptics in the wider culture but from within the theory and especially the institutions of psychoanalysis. Resistance to Freud's vision has been most intense from the other psy-sciences—psychiatry and psychology—in the form of affect theory (particularly as derived from the work of Silvan Tomkins), attachment theory, ego psychology, and of course traumatology—all of which have left their quite distinct imprint on the conceptions of sexuality and subjectivity that animate queer studies.

For reasons explored in chapter 3, we dissent from the way in which John Bowlby and his followers presented attachment theory as a development of psychoanalysis. We see it instead as a parasitic cancellation of Freudian psychoanalysis by normalizing developmental psychology. For Bowlby, intrapsychic conflict is a pathological indicator of failures in the caregiving environment, rather than a typical human predicament. Attachment theory offers a one-dimensional, administrative reduction of psychoanalysis; Bowlby's tacit promise to policy makers was that constitutive human rivenness and the suffering it causes could be eliminated by reordering external reality to produce psychically "secure" citizens. Attachment theory's ideals of subjective coherence and behavioral consistency thus are fundamentally bureaucratic ideals.

We have not offered in this book a comprehensive account of the psy-sciences since Freud, and we are aware that our attempts to map their territory and insist on certain differentiations may seem inadequate. However, we contend that the attempt to map and differentiate is vital for understanding the specific way in which hatred of sex is articulated today, bound up as it is with the expansionist self-aggrandizement of traumatology at the expense of other psy-science theories and therapies. For example, it would be possible to extract from trauma theory a counternarrative, one that depathologizes trauma in certain instances and, indeed, cultivates "traumatophilia" for its psychically productive potential. Through her strikingly original queer reading of Laplanche, psychoanalytic theorist Saketopoulou pursues exactly that project.[5] Our point is that the mainstreaming of traumatology makes such possibilities that much harder to imagine or appreciate.

Thus, we have presented traumatology as a weaponized form of attachment theory that is uniquely adapted to the climate of hypercompetitive individualism characteristic of neoliberal capitalism. The fact that "traumatology" had not hitherto been named testifies to the insidiousness of its influence and the hegemony it enjoys, particularly in Britain and the United States. As a way of thinking and feeling, traumatology now reaches far beyond the clinic and into the wider culture. If its leading practitioners, such as Judith Herman and Bessel van der Kolk, are quite open about their ambitions to reengineer society by excavating hidden histories of abuse wherever they can, they are nevertheless reluctant to take responsibility for any collateral damage, particularly the chilling and intensively normalizing hatred of sex they promote by misconstruing benign sexual inappropriateness as abuse. They fail to acknowledge that victimized identities have become objects of mimetic desire in the social and therapeutic marketplace, whether as lucrative sources of individual redress against institutions, ways of excusing underachievement in a world that judges failure harshly, or as shortcuts to accruing emotional capital within the family circle, in a smash-and-grab raid on the attention and sympathy of anyone who will listen.[6]

Our tactical response to traumatology's expansionist ambitions has been to name the category of benign sexual inappropriateness and insist on its distinction from abuse. We have suggested that the new norm of "appropriateness" performs a similar kind of regulatory work in controlling sexual deviation as the idea of "the normal," and that "queer," defined initially as resistance to the normal, would do well to treat "appropriateness" with comparable skepticism. Attachment theory updated the template of appropriate sexual behavior: infrequent sex in the context of a long-term, secure, amative, intimate, emotionally rich, age-appropriate, and marriage-like relationship. While "inappropriate" sounds more palatable than "abnormal" or "deviant," the stigmatizing antonyms of these standards do the most intensive normalizing work. In some cases "inappropriate behavior" serves as a euphemism for precisely the type of sexual misconduct or abuse that would fall within the scope of criminal law. For anyone working in a position of authority, allegations that they had behaved inappropriately, especially in a sexual sense, would be no small matter. However, in other cases the inappropriate includes all manner of ordinary sexual oddity and awkwardness that is largely benign. This breadth of scope means that the category of the inappropriate, euphemistically evasive about its own normalizing effects, allows ordinarily benign and criminally harmful manifestations of inappropriate sex to be lumped together.

Traumatologists, some of them feminists, may object that there is just no such thing as benign sexual inappropriateness. They may insist that any expression of sexual inappropriateness, if unchallenged, leads to abuse—that sexual inappropriateness is never benign but always an early warning sign of abuse and so cannot be separated from abuse. It might then be objected that what we have called benign sexual inappropriateness is in fact *potential* abuse and therefore that we are dangerously "minimizing" sexual abuse.

The idea that the benign and the harmful exist on a continuum is also assumed by the "epidemiological" approach to tackling sexual abuse on university campuses, an approach enshrined in the proliferating "sex bureaucracies."[7] Sex bureaucracies are engineered to be sensitive to the smallest signs of emergent sexual inappropriateness; they are geared not to recognize any such thing as ordinary sexual inappropriateness that may be benign. Yet, if our claims in this book are correct, then sexual inappropriateness—the violation of propriety in sex, its disordering of the ego and identity—is constitutive of sexual experience. There is no escaping sexual inappropriateness, even when sex is pleasurable and consensual, and thus no escaping our inclination to hate it.

When Gayle Rubin advanced the tactical concept of "benign sexual variation" (on which "benign sexual inappropriateness" is modeled), she was proposing that our understanding of other people's sexual proclivities should begin anthropologically, in the way that we might look upon other cultures by first suspending judgment, rather than viewing them moralistically or with colonialist superiority. Rubin was not attesting that the sexual practices thus surveyed were in themselves all always *absolutely* benign, such that they could never constitute sexual harms we might want to censure, but rather that a happier society would result if our starting assumption were that other people's sexual enjoyment, even when we do not understand or share it, might be *relatively* benign, at least until demonstrated otherwise. In other words, her claims for benign sexual variation tried to de-dramatize the way we initially encounter unfamiliar sexual behavior in others, a temporizing move intended to insert a pause for thought before rushing to moral judgment, a hiatus that would afford the necessary calmness of mind conducive to assessing whether or not harm was really involved. Rubin's tactical concept was not meant to guarantee every unfamiliar sexual practice or scenario as unequivocally harmless. Similarly, while we acknowledge that there will be cases in which benign sexual inappropriateness subsequently morphs into abuse, there are also very many cases in which such inappropriateness never harms anyone.[8]

One obstacle to embracing this view is that today we tend to think "epidemiologically" and algorithmically—to merge our ways of thinking and feeling with the administrative perspective of those monitoring bureaucracies of governance that rule us. In their terms, nothing and nobody is innocent: everyone is a potential sex offender—and every sign of sex is suspect—in the same way that everyone is a potential terrorist. Rather than "minimizing" sexual abuse, our argument for benign sexual inappropriateness is intended to resist the conflation of morally objectionable sexual abuse with those myriad expressions of sexual awkwardness, unwanted attention, sexual unhappiness, and pleasurable excess we have called inappropriateness—a conflation that in our view constitutes the more pervasive and problematic minimization of abuse. By disaggregating these phenomena, we aspire to widen the space between myths of sexual innocence and the assumption of sexual guilt.

The way hatred of sex is experienced today reflects not only the changing ecology of the psy-sciences and economic pressures in the therapeutic marketplace. Today we live in the midst of proliferating algorithmic bureaucracies of governance, all of which aim to identify and monitor risk from the moment of its emergence. Since these bureaucracies are designed to enable preemptive action to ensure the security of the society and subjects concerned, it is indeed the case that, from their perspective, all sex is potentially abuse and should be tracked as such. Our category of benign sexual inappropriateness holds no meaning within the bureaucratic frame of such thinking and for that reason is all the more necessary a corrective. Just as time and death are alien to the unconscious, so too we might say is making proportionate judgments about risk.

For the unconscious, as for the algorithm and the traumatologist, it would seem that even small risks are substantial and may constitute motives for action. Bureaucracies of governance consolidate and exploit this propensity to misjudge even small risks of potential future harms by conflating the mere possibility of harm with the probability of harm. As our social and political institutions—universities among them—are reengineered to remove any possibility for discretion and dissent, in an ongoing global proletarianization of middle-class labor, sex bureaucracies are in the vanguard of this administrative and technocratic stealth revolution: their insistence on the "proper processes" teaches a much wider cultural and institutional lesson by leveraging the human hatred of sex.

Although Trump has left the White House, Trumpism—the populist *ressentiment* of the deplorables with their injured white-supremacist identity—looks set to stay. And indeed, the world is awash with authoritarian populist leaders of similar ilk: Jair Bolsonaro, Mohammed bin Salman, Recep Tayyip Erdoğan, Boris Johnson, Narendra Modi, Viktor Orbán, and Vladimir Putin, to name a few. It is worth reflecting on this new populism and how the ground was prepared for it. We suggest that it may be these rulers' flamboyant disregard for process, propriety, and appropriateness, at a time when these are becoming so rigidly constraining a part of daily life under algorithmic and trauma-tological rule, that partly explains their charismatic appeal, at least to their base. For all its deplorability, this base nonetheless recognizes that there is something stifling and unlivable about the impersonal bureaucratic rule of "governance," about a world hygienically purged of disagreement and inappropriateness. Much of the progressive Left, particularly in the United States, has placed its faith in those bureaucracies to make progress toward equality across various axes of difference. However, the populism of the inappropriate returns with a vengeance in what we now are tempted to call the Trumpenproletariat.

When Friedrich Engels first invoked the *Lumpenproletariat*, in 1846, it was as a politically vicious ragbag of depravity that lay beneath the proletariat and threatened to undermine it.[9] He and Karl Marx incorporated the term into their famous manifesto two years later, sneering as they did so at this "'dangerous class,' the social scum, that passively rotting mass thrown off by the lowest layers of old society" and susceptible to being used as "a bribed tool of reactionary intrigue."[10] The term was redeployed and its meaning substantially complicated in Marx's study of the right-wing coup d'état by Louis-Napoléon Bonaparte in 1851, an analysis of the conditions in which "a grotesque medioc-rity came to play a hero's part."[11] We are not the first to notice parallels between the Bonaparte coup and Trump's ascendancy to the highest public office of the United States; it would take another book to explore them adequately. Most significant for our purposes is that Marxist science, in its invention of the lumpenproletariat, not only replicated the governing classes' structural division of the working class into the respectable and the residuum—the former being susceptible to moralizing rule, while the latter were irredeemable, unfit for anything but policing and containment—but also reproduced their sneering contempt for those thereby consigned to the dustbin category in their theory of proletarian revolution.[12] The "Lumpen" named one part of a division that weighed heavily upon the entire century, as historian Michelle Perrot observes, including for Marx and Engels.[13] From Rancière's perspective, a cognate sneering has contaminated the structural categories not just of Marxism and democratic socialism but also of ostensibly more moderate center-left political analysis ever since, as his account of the storming of the Capitol indicates.[14]

E. P. Thompson once suggested that in the late eighteenth century the crowd appeared to the great and the good "through the haze of verdure surrounding their parks, to be made up of 'the loose and disorderly sort.'"[15] This disdainful apprehension of the crowd—the mob, the rabble, the multitude, the unwashed masses, the lumpenproletariat—has its own passionately inegalitarian history, to which Hillary Clinton appended her codicil of contempt for the "deplorables," sneering down at them as if from her gilded Goldman Sachs lectern. That her remark should be inscribed within this lineage can be discerned from the fuller expression of Clinton's disdain—the "basket of deplorables"—that emphasized the heteroclite jumble of this flotsam and jetsam, the disorderliness of the assortment. The Trumpenproletariat, Clinton implies, is a disorderly ragbag, an affront not only to egalitarian values (in its disregard for women and minorities) but also to the analytical seriousness of progressive political science.

By sneering at the Trumpenproletariat, Clinton gave grist to their mill, helping to consolidate what in sociological terms was a highly improbable alliance between a reality TV star, wealthy Republican donors, petit bourgeois cryptofascists, and the mainly white working class. Yet, as Rancière reminds us, Trumpism cannot be fully explained sociologically, in terms of the frustration of those "left behind," but rather stems from a "system of affects that is not intended for any particular class and which plays not on frustration but, on the contrary, on satisfaction with one's condition, not on a feeling of inequality to be repaired but on a feeling of privilege to be maintained."[16] Rancière identifies the Trumpenproletariat as motivated by the "passion for inequality," an eagerness to embrace its own form of sneering superiority over "a multitude of inferiors": women, ethnic minorities, trans people, Muslims, Mexicans, experts, Democrats, and so on.[17] Progressive political analysts who have tried to explain the Trumpenproletariat only in terms of their *ressentiment*-ridden reaction to being left behind by global capitalism were taken in by their tactical ploy—that is, by cynical political mimicry of the Left's attachment to injured identity and its displacement onto white working-class identity. The fact of the matter is that the Trumpenproletariat and those who take such pleasure in deploring them are all afflicted by hatred of democracy.

Intertwined with these different ways of hating the disorderliness of democracy has been a persistent hatred of sex. Marx famously characterized the lumpenproletariat thus: "Alongside decayed roués with dubious means of subsistence and of dubious origin, alongside ruined and adventurous offshoots of the bourgeoisie, were vagabonds, discharged soldiers, discharged jailbirds, escaped galley slaves, swindlers, mountebanks, lazzaroni, pickpockets, tricksters, gamblers, *maquereaux*, brothel keepers, porters, literati, organ grinders, ragpickers, knife grinders, tinkers, beggars—in short, the whole indefinite, dis-integrated mass, thrown hither and thither, which the French call *la bohème*."[18] Note the presence, in this disorderly ragbag, of what are likely syphilitic sex addicts born out of wedlock ("decayed roués . . . of dubious origin"), panderers, brothel keepers, and pleasure-loving "bohemians": hatred of sex lends Marx's heterogeneous dustbin category perhaps its only plausible coherence. At first glance the Trumpenproletariat that stormed the Capitol looked very different, though almost as heteroclite: convicted criminals, off-duty police officers, Republican Party officials, members of a panoply of far-right militias (including neo-Nazis), and members of the armed forces. With them, how-ever, were evangelical Christians, doctors, lawyers, CEOs and entrepreneurs, IT workers, accountants, and "middle-aged, middle-class insurrectionists," not to mention a vegan, white-supremacist, self-proclaimed shaman.[19] Although Rancière dismissed as merely "delusional" this Trumpenproletariat's unifying commitment to the QAnon conspiracy-theory belief that their savior had come to purge the world of blood-sucking pedophiles, we disagree with his view. On the contrary, this conspiracy theory must be understood as downdraft from the crushing cross-party consensus of the 1990s, which gave birth to sexual predator legislation. Inspired by hatred of sex and hatred of democracy, that consensus had already signaled the collapse of representative democracy.

The Trumpenproletariat's protofascist insurgency and the ongoing reaction against it thus suggest that representative democracy in the United States is at a crossroads defined by the interlocking of hatred of sex with hatred of democracy. Center-left politicians and analysts would further attenuate the lingering remnants of radical democracy within that system, absorbing its disturbing disorderliness into a bureaucratic-technocratic administration—governance without politics—that supposedly would better safeguard already recognized minorities with authorized grievances and secure the nation from full-fledged fascism. Conversely, the Trumpenproletariat would transform the political system into a police state in which the rhetoric of "law and order" provides cover for vicious legal and extralegal attacks on minorities, immigrants, experts, women's rights—essentially, Gilead.[20] Both sides hate democracy and both hate sex; both hate the disorder of sex and the disorder of democracy; one side hates the disorder of sexual "inappropriateness," and the other hates benign sexual variation. Both want an even less radically democratic political system that reflects only their own priorities. Lest we be misunderstood, our claim is not that these various causes on either side deserve equal respect from some purely notional third vantage point but that the grievances and the communities that form around them are always political matters. These matters need to be engaged politically in a spirit of radical democracy and radical equality, rather than being projected out of the dissensual sphere of politics into a realm of suprapolitical consensus or contained within sneering, sociologistic, pseudoscientific wisdom.

Populism functions by designating certain issues as suprapolitical, beyond the disagreement and debate of ordinary politics. Representative (or liberal) democracy can be understood as occupying a midpoint between radical democracy and the suppression of politics that has been variously named "totalitarianism" and "governance." In U.S. domestic politics of the 1990s, hatred of sex and hatred of democracy were intertwined in mutually supporting ways, as we witnessed the development of an intractable cross-party consensus around sexual predator legislation and the "right-to-know" approach to released sex offenders. This antisexual populism was already a way of short-circuiting liberal democracy and collapsing it onto the governance pole, meaning the pole at which there is no room for disagreement—for politics, as Rancière defines it—because *there must be consensus* around issues of such importance.

This sexual populism, which suited the melodramatic imperatives of media reporting, prepared the ground for the antiterrorist security populism that succeeded it. Little wonder that millions of QAnon followers believe the world has been taken over by a cabal of predatory pedophiles. The absence of any empirical evidence for this global pedophilic network is entirely beside the point, since QAnon is a fantasy that coheres at the level of psychic reality (not external reality) and thereby galvanizes those who are happy to share it.[21] Doubtless the aftereffects of these populisms—and the systems of bureaucratic monitoring they spawned—will be with us for many years to come. In this book we have tried to carve out some space for genuinely critical reflection on their ramifications, as well as to cast some light on hatred of sex.

NOTES

1. HATRED OF SEX

1. Rancière, *Hatred of Democracy*, 6.
2. Rancière, *Hatred of Democracy*, 2.
3. J. Dean, *Democracy and Other Neoliberal Fantasies*.
4. Crépon, Cassin, and Moatti, "People/Race/Nation," 760.
5. This once ubiquitous phrase was coined in 1830 by the Victorian novelist Edward Bulwer-Lytton.
6. For an acute critique of presidentialism, see Nelson, *Bad for Democracy*; and for a critical history of the Electoral College, see Keyssar, *Why Do We Still Have the Electoral College?*
7. Nelson, *Commons Democracy*, 6.
8. Nelson, *Commons Democracy*, 175.
9. Nelson, "Democracy in Theory," 86.
10. See Hardt and Negri, *Multitude*; Hardt and Negri, *Commonwealth*; Virno, *Grammar of the Multitude*; and Casarino and Negri, *In Praise of the Common*.
11. Virno, *Grammar of the Multitude*, 21 (original emphases).
12. Hardt and Negri, *Multitude*, xi.
13. Quoted in Chozick, "Hillary Clinton Calls Many Trump Backers 'Deplorables,'" A18.
14. Blow, "About the 'Basket of Deplorables,'" A23.
15. Rancière, *Disagreement*.
16. On the leftist case for Brexit, see Tuck, *Left Case for Brexit*; and Whyman, *Left Case for Brexit*. For critiques of the European Union

as bad for democracy, see Dardot and Laval, *Ce cauchemar qui n'en finit pas*; and Lapavitsas, *Left Case against the EU*.

17. Hazeley and Morris, *Story of Brexit*, 28.

18. S. Freud, "Antithetical Meaning of Primal Words," 159.

19. S. Freud, "Antithetical Meaning of Primal Words," 155, 156.

20. S. Freud, "The Unconscious," 186.

21. Agamben, *Homo Sacer*, 78.

22. Rancière, *Hatred of Democracy*, 76.

23. Foucault, "Interview by Stephen Riggins," 129.

24. Our argument in this part of the chapter builds on, as well as revises, T. Dean, "Biopolitics of Pleasure"; and T. Dean, "Foucault and Sex."

25. Foucault, *History of Sexuality*, 1:157.

26. Michel Foucault, "The Culture of the Self" (unpublished seminar), quoted in Schuster, *Trouble with Pleasure*, 97.

27. S. Freud, "Instincts and Their Vicissitudes," 135.

28. S. Freud, *Three Essays on the Theory of Sexuality*, 209.

29. S. Freud, *Three Essays on the Theory of Sexuality*, 209 (translation modified).

30. S. Freud, "Instincts and Their Vicissitudes," 136 (punctuation modified).

31. A. Freud, *Ego and the Mechanisms of Defence*.

32. S. Freud, *Three Essays on the Theory of Sexuality*, 135n2.

33. Translator's note in S. Freud, *Three Essays on the Theory of Sexuality*, 135n2.

34. Deleuze, "Desire and Pleasure."

35. Schuster, *Trouble with Pleasure*, 197n12.

36. S. Freud, *Civilization and Its Discontents*, 108–9.

37. S. Freud, *Beyond the Pleasure Principle*, 50.

38. S. Freud, *Civilization and Its Discontents*, 108.

39. Laplanche and Pontalis, *Language of Psycho-Analysis*, 153.

40. Laplanche, *Life and Death in Psychoanalysis*, 123 (original emphasis).

41. Foucault, *History of Sexuality*, 1:155.

42. Schuster, *Trouble with Pleasure*, 115.

43. Schuster, *Trouble with Pleasure*, 101.

44. Schuster, *Trouble with Pleasure*, 106–7. The Freud quotations are from his *Beyond the Pleasure Principle*, 11.

45. See Phillips, *Unforbidden Pleasures.*
46. S. Freud, *Beyond the Pleasure Principle*, 63.
47. S. Freud, *Beyond the Pleasure Principle*, 63.
48. Foucault, *History of Sexuality*, 1:157.
49. This distinction is missing from Sophie Fontanel's popular memoir, *The Art of Sleeping Alone.*
50. S. Freud, *Civilization and Its Discontents*, 114.
51. S. Freud, *Civilization and Its Discontents*, 114.
52. This phrase appears in the subtitle of Michaels, *Trouble with Diversity.*
53. Orwell, *Animal Farm*, chap. 10.
54. Rancière, *Hatred of Democracy*, 47.
55. Rancière, *Hatred of Democracy*, 49 (emphasis added).
56. S. Freud, "A Difficulty in the Path of Psycho-Analysis," 143.
57. Phillips, *Equals*, 13.
58. Phillips, *Equals*, 16.
59. S. Freud, *The Question of Lay Analysis.*
60. Mouffe, *The Democratic Paradox*, 103.
61. See S. Freud, "Analysis Terminable and Interminable."
62. De Botton, *How to Think More about Sex*, 4.
63. See Scott, *Extravagant Abjection.*
64. Saketopoulou, "Risking Sexuality beyond Consent," 785.

2. DOES QUEER STUDIES HATE SEX?

1. Rubin, "Thinking Sex," 267. For the canonization, see Abelove, Barale, and Halperin, *Lesbian and Gay Studies Reader*, 3–44. Donald E. Hall and Annamarie Jagose declined to reprint "Thinking Sex" in *The Routledge Queer Studies Reader* in 2013 because it is "already widely available in other anthologies" (xviii) and thus canonical.
2. Eng, Halberstam, and Muñoz, "What's Queer about Queer Studies Now?," 2.
3. Eng, Halberstam, and Muñoz, "What's Queer about Queer Studies Now?," 2.
4. Rubin, "Thinking Sex," 275.
5. Rubin, "Thinking Sex," 277.
6. "Thinking Sex" had its debut at the Scholar and the Feminist IX Conference, held at Barnard College, New York City, on April 24, 1982; the conference theme was "Towards a Politics of Sexuality."

7. Rubin, "Thinking Sex," 307.

8. Sedgwick, *Epistemology of the Closet*, 16.

9. Halley, *Split Decisions*, 25.

10. Halley, *Split Decisions*, 35 (emphasis added).

11. See Duggan and Hunter, *Sex Wars*.

12. See SAMOIS, *Coming to Power*.

13. Rubin, "Thinking Sex," 283. Benign sexual variation was a key concept for Tim Dean's *Unlimited Intimacy*, but we are complicating it here.

14. Rubin, "Thinking Sex," 283.

15. Rubin, "Thinking Sex," 308.

16. Rubin, "Thinking Sex," 309.

17. Rubin, "Blood under the Bridge," 217, 218.

18. Rubin, "Thinking Sex," 308.

19. Rubin, "Thinking Sex," 293.

20. Rostom Mesli argues that Rubin's is the more politically radical perspective, precisely because it respects the relative autonomy of sex from gender, race, class, ethnicity, ability, and so on. See Mesli, "Gayle Rubin's Concept of 'Benign Sexual Variation.'"

21. Halley, *Split Decisions*, 25–26. Given that intersectionality exemplifies convergentism, it is surprising that Halley does not discuss it, or mention Crenshaw, in *Split Decisions*.

22. Eng, Halberstam, and Muñoz, "What's Queer about Queer Studies Now?," 1.

23. Crenshaw, "Demarginalizing the Intersection of Race and Sex," 139.

24. Crenshaw, "Demarginalizing the Intersection of Race and Sex," 146.

25. Civil Rights Act of 1964, § 7, 42 U.S.C. § 2000e et seq. (1964).

26. Bostock v. Clayton County, 590 U.S. _ (more) 140 S. Ct. 1731; 2020 WL 3146686; 2020 U.S. LEXIS 3252.

27. Wiegman, *Object Lessons*, 299.

28. Benjamin Weil, roundtable comment at Viral Masculinities conference, University of Exeter, September 4, 2020.

29. Boellstorff, "Sexualities 2038," 1386.

30. Wiegman, *Object Lessons*, 31.

31. Wiegman, *Object Lessons*, 242.

32. Moi, *Revolution of the Ordinary*, 106.

33. Wittgenstein, *Blue and Brown Books*, 17.

34. Moi, *Revolution of the Ordinary*, 96 (original emphases).

35. Moi, *Revolution of the Ordinary*, 100.

36. See Nash, "Intersectionality and Its Discontents"; Nash, *Black Feminism Reimagined*; and Puar, *Terrorist Assemblages*.

37. See, for example, Crenshaw, "Demarginalizing the Intersection of Race and Sex," 139.

38. Ferguson, *One-Dimensional Queer*, 12.

39. Ferguson, *One-Dimensional Queer*, 7.

40. Crenshaw, "Mapping the Margins," 1244 (original emphasis).

41. Crenshaw, "Mapping the Margins," 1265–82.

42. Bersani, "Is the Rectum a Grave?," 197.

43. For example, neither Abelove, Barale, and Halperin's *Lesbian and Gay Studies Reader* (1993) nor Hall and Jagose's *Routledge Queer Studies Reader* (2013) includes "Is the Rectum a Grave?" Johnson and Henderson's compendious *Black Queer Studies* (2005) never mentions Bersani (or Rubin). For the claim that Bersani's contributions to queer theory have been essentially traumatic, see T. Dean, "Sex and the Aesthetics of Existence," 387.

44. For a full-scale analysis of Bersani as an ontologist, see Tuhkanen, *Essentialist Villain*.

45. Bersani, "Is the Rectum a Grave?," 201 (original emphasis).

46. See K. Davis, "Intersectionality as Buzzword."

47. Treichler, *How to Have Theory in an Epidemic*, 50–51.

48. Bersani, "Is the Rectum a Grave?," 198 (original emphasis).

49. Rubin, "Thinking Sex," 298.

50. Bersani, "Is the Rectum a Grave?," 215.

51. Bersani, "Is the Rectum a Grave?," 217.

52. Bersani, "Is the Rectum a Grave?," 217.

53. Bersani, "Is the Rectum a Grave?," 217.

54. S. Freud, *Three Essays on the Theory of Sexuality*, 135.

55. Bersani, "Is the Rectum a Grave?," 222.

56. Bersani, "Is the Rectum a Grave?," 222.

57. See Stockton, *Beautiful Bottom, Beautiful Shame*; Scott, *Extravagant Abjection*; Nguyen, *View from the Bottom*; Foltz, *Contemporary American Literature and Excremental Culture*; Saketopoulou, "Risking Sexuality beyond Consent"; and Saketopoulou, "Draw to Overwhelm."

58. Bersani, "Is the Rectum a Grave?," 222.

59. See the text of Harris, *Slave Play*; and also Saketopoulou, "Sexuality beyond Consent."

60. S. Freud, *Three Essays on the Theory of Sexuality*, 152–53.

61. Green, *Chains of Eros*, 6.

62. Dimen, *Surviving Sexual Contradictions*, 17.

63. Dimen, *Surviving Sexual Contradictions*, 18.

64. Green, *Chains of Eros*, 12.

65. S. Freud, *Three Essays on the Theory of Sexuality*, 203.

66. S. Freud, *Drei Abhandlungen zur Sexualtheorie*, 104.

67. S. Freud, *Three Essays on the Theory of Sexuality*, 203–4.

68. Laplanche, *Life and Death in Psychoanalysis*, 101 (original emphasis).

69. Green, *Chains of Eros*, 18. We note that Hinshelwood, *Dictionary of Kleinian Thought*, contains no entry under "pleasure."

70. Laplanche, *Temptation of Biology*, 111.

71. Laplanche, *Temptation of Biology*, 111.

72. Sedgwick, "Paranoid Reading and Reparative Reading," 128ff.

73. See Ricoeur, *Freud and Philosophy*, 32–36.

74. See Jameson, *Political Unconscious*.

75. See Latour, "Why Has Critique Run Out of Steam?"

76. Klein, "Mourning and Its Relation to Manic-Depressive States," 350–51.

77. Deleuze, "Desire and Pleasure," 189.

78. Tomkins, *Shame and Its Sisters*, 49.

79. Sedgwick, *Touching Feeling*, 13.

80. Leys, *From Guilt to Shame*, 191. See also Leys, "The Turn to Affect," which elaborates an especially strong critique of Tomkins and his uptake by Sedgwick.

81. Foucault, "Sex, Power, and the Politics of Identity," 165.

82. Foucault, "Sex, Power, and the Politics of Identity," 165 (original emphases).

83. S. Freud, *Three Essays on the Theory of Sexuality*, 194.

84. S. Freud, *Drei Abhandlungen zur Sexualtheorie*, 95.

85. See Salecl, *Passion for Ignorance*.

86. Laplanche, *Temptation of Biology*, 9.

3. SECURING THE APPROPRIATE

1. Rancière, *Hatred of Democracy*, 2, 36.

2. Rancière, *Hatred of Democracy*, 1, 37.

3. Rancière, *Hatred of Democracy*, 37.

4. Rancière, *Hatred of Democracy*, 47.

5. Rubin, "Thinking Sex," 278.

6. Brown, *Undoing the Demos*, 123; O. Davis, "Neoliberal Capitalism's Bureaucracies of 'Governance.'"

7. For a synoptic overview, see Halley et al., *Governance Feminism*.

8. Bernstein, "Militarized Humanitarianism Meets Carceral Feminism."

9. Gottschalk, *Prison and the Gallows*, 9.

10. Lamble, "Queer Necropolitics and the Expanding Carceral State."

11. Spade, *Normal Life*, xii.

12. Halperin and Hoppe, *War on Sex*, 13–14.

13. Levine, "Sympathy for the Devil," 129.

14. Mansnerus, "For What They Might Do," 285.

15. Lancaster, "New Pariahs," 85.

16. Lancaster, "New Pariahs," 85. See also Lancaster, *Sex Panic and the Punitive State*, 100.

17. Brown, *Undoing the Demos*, 36.

18. Brown, *States of Injury*, 21.

19. Jenkins, *Moral Panic*, 127.

20. Gottschalk, *Prison and the Gallows*, 84.

21. Bumiller, *In an Abusive State*, 7.

22. Jenkins, *Moral Panic*, 118.

23. Jenkins, *Moral Panic*, 119.

24. Fischel, *Screw Consent*, 118.

25. MacKinnon, *Feminism Unmodified*, 82.

26. Best, "Victimization and the Victim Industry," 13.

27. Rouvroy and Berns, "Algorithmic Governmentality and Prospects of Emancipation."

28. Rubin, "Thinking Sex," 281.

29. Contratto, "Feminist Critique of Attachment Theory and Evolutionary Psychology," 30.

30. Bowlby, *Attachment and Loss*, 1:xi; van Dijken, *John Bowlby*, 78, 84.

31. Van der Horst and van der Veer, "Separation and Divergence," 244.

32. Van Dijken, *John Bowlby*, 62, 68.

33. Bowlby, *Attachment and Loss*, 2:210.

34. Bowlby, *Attachment and Loss*, 1:5, 337.

35. Bowlby, *Attachment and Loss*, 2:253.

36. Bowlby, *Attachment and Loss*, 1:358.

37. Contratto, "Feminist Critique of Attachment Theory and Evolutionary Psychology," 32.

38. Fear, *Attachment Theory*, 48.

39. Marcuse, *One-Dimensional Man*, 12 (original emphasis).

40. Van Dijken, *John Bowlby*, 85.

41. Bowlby, *Forty-Four Juvenile Thieves*, 3, 6.

42. Bowlby, *Forty-Four Juvenile Thieves*, 6.

43. Bowlby, *Forty-Four Juvenile Thieves*, 54.

44. Green, "Has Sexuality Anything to Do with Psychoanalysis?," 873.

45. Green, "Has Sexuality Anything to Do with Psychoanalysis?," 877; Rancière, *Disagreement*; Rancière, *Politics of Aesthetics*.

46. Bowlby, *Attachment and Loss*, 1:5.

47. Van Dijken, *John Bowlby*, 136; Shapira, *War Inside*, 16.

48. Holmes, *John Bowlby and Attachment Theory*, 15.

49. Bowlby quoted in van Dijken, *John Bowlby*, 3 (original ellipses).

50. Bowlby, *Attachment and Loss*, 2:370.

51. It has been suggested that Bowlby's antipsychoanalytic determinism about the effects of separation caused a rift with one of his closest early collaborators, James Robertson. Van der Horst and van der Veer, "Separation and Divergence," 248.

52. Holland, "Representing Children in Child Protection Assessments," 331–34.

53. Bowlby, *Attachment and Loss*, 2:26. The first of these films was *A Two-Year-Old Goes to Hospital* (1952).

54. Miller and Rose, *Governing the Present*, 9.

55. Bowlby, *Attachment and Loss*, 1:17–18.

56. Bowlby, *Attachment and Loss*, 1:18, 83, 104–5.

57. Bowlby, *Attachment and Loss*, 1:205, 207, 2:130.

58. Bowlby, *Attachment and Loss*, 1:346.

59. Van Dijken, *John Bowlby*, 150; Bowlby, *Attachment and Loss*, 1:362.

60. Contratto, "Feminist Critique of Attachment Theory and Evolutionary Psychology," 30.

61. Bowlby, *Attachment and Loss*, 1:362.

62. Fear, *Attachment Theory*, 144.

63. Bowlby, *Attachment and Loss*, 1:337.

64. Bowlby, *Secure Base*, 11.

65. Bowlby, *Attachment and Loss*, 2:94.

66. Bowlby, *Secure Base*, 140.

67. Bowlby, *Attachment and Loss*, 1:337; Bretherton, "Origins of Attachment Theory," 760; Ainsworth, "Security and Attachment," 43, 44–46, 52.

68. Ainsworth, "Security and Attachment," 52.

69. Van Rosmalen and van der Horst, "From Secure Dependency to Attachment," 36–37.

70. Blatz, *Human Security*, 114–15.

71. Blatz, *Human Security*, 63.

72. Bowlby, *Attachment and Loss*, 2:213.

73. Van der Kolk, "John Bowlby Memorial Lecture 2006," 48.

74. Miller and Rose, *Governing the Present*, 146.

75. Miller and Rose, *Governing the Present*, 142–72.

76. Bowlby, *Attachment and Loss*, 1:54–55.

77. Bowlby, *Attachment and Loss*, 1:61.

78. Bowlby, *Attachment and Loss*, 1:55.

79. Bowlby, *Attachment and Loss*, 2:82 (original emphasis).

80. Bowlby, *Attachment and Loss*, 1:59.

81. Bowlby, *Attachment and Loss*, 1:60.

82. Bowlby, *Attachment and Loss*, 1:151.

83. Bowlby, *Attachment and Loss*, 1:130–31.

84. Duschinsky, Greco, and Solomon, "Wait Up!," 223–25; Yellin, "Such Stuff as Dreams Are Made On."

85. Bowlby, *Attachment and Loss*, 1:60.

86. Bowlby, *Attachment and Loss*, 1:224, 226.

87. Bowlby, *Secure Base*, 78.

88. Bowlby, *Attachment and Loss*, 1:63.

89. Jenkins, *Moral Panic*, 193–94.

4. TRAUMATOLOGY AND GOVERNANCE

1. Herman, *Trauma and Recovery*, 51–52.

2. Herman, *Trauma and Recovery*, 102–3.

3. Herman, *Trauma and Recovery*, 34.

4. Herman, *Trauma and Recovery*, 37, 156.

5. Herman, *Trauma and Recovery*, 157.

6. Herman, *Trauma and Recovery*, 75, 141.

7. Herman, *Trauma and Recovery*, 30.

8. Herman, *Trauma and Recovery*, 158.

9. Suleiman, "Judith Herman and Contemporary Trauma Theory," 278.

10. Suleiman, "Judith Herman and Contemporary Trauma Theory," 278; Herman, *Trauma and Recovery*, 158.

11. Suleiman, "Judith Herman and Contemporary Trauma Theory," 278 (original emphasis).

12. Jenkins, *Moral Panic*, 183–84.

13. Loftus and Pickrell, "Formation of False Memories," 725.

14. Herman, *Trauma and Recovery*, 3.

15. Herman, *Trauma and Recovery*, 158.

16. Borch-Jacobsen, "Neurotica," 33 (original emphasis).

17. Herman, *Trauma and Recovery*, 146.

18. Herman, *Trauma and Recovery*, 144–45.

19. La Fontaine, *Speak of the Devil*, 103.

20. La Fontaine, *Speak of the Devil*, 98–99.

21. La Fontaine, *Speak of the Devil*, 99.

22. La Fontaine, *Speak of the Devil*, 99.

23. La Fontaine, *Speak of the Devil*, 105.

24. Sinason and Hale, *Pilot Study on Alleged Organised Ritual Abuse*, 9.

25. Epstein, Schwartz, and Schwartz, *Ritual Abuse and Mind Control*, 5.

26. Sinason, "What Has Changed in Twenty Years?," 22.

27. Sinason, "What Has Changed in Twenty Years?," 28 (emphasis added).

28. Sinason, "What Has Changed in Twenty Years?," 28.

29. Sinason, "What Has Changed in Twenty Years?," 55–56.

30. Sinason, "What Has Changed in Twenty Years?," 55.

31. Sinason, "What Has Changed in Twenty Years?," 57.

32. Sinason, "What Has Changed in Twenty Years?," 58.

33. Sinason, "What Has Changed in Twenty Years?," 69.

34. La Fontaine, *Speak of the Devil*, 106.

35. Schwartz, "'Evil Cradling?,'" 91 (emphasis added).

36. Schwartz, "'Evil Cradling?,'" 87 (emphasis added).

37. Lacter, "Torture-Based Mind Control," 102.

38. Lacter, "Torture-Based Mind Control," 147 (emphasis added).

39. Lacter, "Torture-Based Mind Control," 169.

40. Epstein, "Working with the Incredible Hulk," 240 (emphasis added).

41. Storr, "Mystery of Carole Myers."

42. Herman, *Trauma and Recovery*, 140.

43. Levack, *Witch-Hunt in Early Modern Europe*, 174.

44. Herman, *Trauma and Recovery*, 118.

45. Herman, *Trauma and Recovery*, 135.

46. Best, "Victimization and the Victim Industry," 10.

47. Jenkins, *Moral Panic*, 218.

48. Herman, *Trauma and Recovery*, 128.

49. Herman, *Trauma and Recovery*, 148.

50. Keane quoted in Herman, *Trauma and Recovery*, 148.

51. Davies, *Limits of Neoliberalism*, 29, 30.

52. Lancaster, "New Pariahs," 76.

53. Bröckling, *Entrepreneurial Self*.

54. Leys, *Trauma*, 6.

55. Leys, *Trauma*, 263–65.

56. Leys, *Trauma*, 264–65.

57. Leys, *Trauma*, 266.

58. Leys, *Trauma*, 305, 237, respectively.

59. Van der Kolk and Greenberg, "Psychobiology of the Trauma Response," 71.

60. Leys, *Trauma*, 257.

61. Leys, *Trauma*, 257. See also van der Kolk and Greenberg, "Psychobiology of the Trauma Response," 63–64.

AFTERWORD

1. Rancière, "Fools and the Wise."

2. Hofstadter, *Paranoid Style in American Politics*.

3. Green, *Chains of Eros*, 2.

4. Fischel, *Sex and Harm in the Age of Consent*; Saketopoulou, "Risking Sexuality beyond Consent."

5. Saketopoulou, *Risking Sexuality beyond Consent*, chap. 4.

6. See Brown, *States of Injury*, chap. 3.

7. See Gersen and Gersen, "Sex Bureaucracy."

8. For a host of examples of benign sexual inappropriateness, see Delany, *Times Square Red, Times Square Blue*.

9. Dominique Kalifa suggests that the concept has a racist-colonialist genealogy, insofar as Engels derived it from his experience of the impoverished Irish subproletariat in Manchester in 1842. Kalifa, *Les bas-fonds*, 120–21.

10. Marx and Engels, *Manifesto of the Communist Party*.

11. Marx, *Eighteenth Brumaire of Louis Bonaparte*. The complications of the term's meaning were so intense and varied that it has remained something of an enigma within Marxist political theory ever since. In the extensive scholarly literature devoted to untangling its meaning, see especially Hayes, "Utopia and the Lumpenproletariat"; Stallybrass, "Marx and Heterogeneity"; and Bourdin, "Marx et le Lumpenprolétariat." What all of these accounts miss is the bilingual German-English complication. In German *Lumpen* meant rags—Engels was talking first of all about the very poor, dressed only in rags, as in the homeless and destitute—yet as the term is taken up by these polyglot theorists it interferes with the English "lump," more as verb than as noun: the disorderly, heteroclite jumble Marx lists in *The Eighteenth Brumaire* is literally "lumped together."

12. The structural necessity of the category in their elaboration of Marxist science is noted in Bourdin, "Marx et le Lumpenprolétariat," 43, echoing the critique in Rancière's *The Philosopher and His Poor* of Marxist scientism and its legacy in sociology. This dustbin category served the needs of Marxist *science*: how to resolve the enigma of a fraction of the working class that repeatedly acted against its class interest and that could not be converted to the cause of proletarian revolution but enlisted only in its violent suppression.

13. Perrot, "1848 révolution et prisons," 316.

14. Rancière, "Fools and the Wise."

15. Thompson, *Customs in Common*, 35.

16. Rancière, "Fools and the Wise."

17. Rancière, "Fools and the Wise."

18. Marx, *Eighteenth Brumaire*, 241.
19. Pape and Ruby, "Capitol Rioters Aren't Like Other Extremists."
20. Gilead is the dystopia depicted in *The Handmaid's Tale*, Margaret Atwood's 1985 novel.
21. See Rubenstein, *This Is Not a President*.

BIBLIOGRAPHY

Abelove, Henry, Michèle Aina Barale, and David M. Halperin, eds. *The Lesbian and Gay Studies Reader*. New York: Routledge, 1993.

Agamben, Giorgio. *Homo Sacer: Sovereign Power and Bare Life*. Translated by Daniel Heller-Roazen. Stanford CA: Stanford University Press, 1998.

Ainsworth, Mary Salter. "Security and Attachment." In *The Secure Child: Timeless Lessons in Parenting and Childhood Education*, edited by Richard Volpe, 43–53. Charlotte NC: Information Age, 2010.

Atwood, Margaret. *The Handmaid's Tale*. 1985. New York: Penguin, 1998.

Bartholet, Elizabeth, Nancy Gertner, Janet Halley, and Jeannie Suk Gersen. "Fairness for All Students under Title IX." Harvard Library Office for Scholarly Communication, August 21, 2017. http://nrs.harvard.edu/urn-3:HUL.InstRepos:33789434.

Berlant, Lauren, and Lee Edelman. *Sex, or the Unbearable*. Durham NC: Duke University Press, 2014.

Bernstein, Elizabeth. "Militarized Humanitarianism Meets Carceral Feminism: The Politics of Sex, Rights, and Freedom in Contemporary Anti-Trafficking Campaigns." In "Feminists Theorize International Political Economy," edited by Shirin M. Rai and Kate Bedford. Special issue, *Signs: Journal of Women in Culture and Society* 36, no. 1 (2010): 45–71.

Bersani, Leo. *Homos*. Cambridge MA: Harvard University Press, 1995.

———. "Is the Rectum a Grave?" In *AIDS: Cultural Analysis/Cultural Activism*, edited by Douglas Crimp, 197–222. Cambridge MA: MIT Press, 1988.

Best, Joel. "Victimization and the Victim Industry." *Society* 34, no. 4 (1997): 9–17.

Blatz, William. *Human Security: Some Reflections*. London: University of London Press, 1967.

Blow, Charles M. "About the 'Basket of Deplorables.'" *New York Times*, September 11, 2016.

Boellstorff, Tom. "Sexualities 2038." *Sexualities* 21, no. 8 (2018): 1385–88.

Borch-Jacobsen, Mikkel. "Neurotica: Freud and the Seduction Theory." *October* 76 (Spring 1996): 15–43.

Bourdin, Jean-Claude. "Marx et le Lumpenprolétariat." *Actuel Marx* 54, no. 2 (2013): 39–55.

Bowlby, John. *Attachment and Loss*. Vol. 1, *Attachment*. 2nd ed. London: Hogarth Press and the Institute of Psycho-Analysis, 1982.

———. *Attachment and Loss*. Vol. 2, *Separation. Anger and Anxiety*. London: Hogarth Press and the Institute of Psycho-Analysis, 1973.

———. *Forty-Four Juvenile Thieves: Their Characters and Home-Life*. London: Baillière, Tindall & Cox, 1946.

———. *A Secure Base: Clinical Applications of Attachment Theory*. 1989. London: Routledge, 1998.

Bretherton, Inge. "The Origins of Attachment Theory: John Bowlby and Mary Ainsworth." *Developmental Psychology* 28, no. 5 (1992): 759–75.

Bröckling, Ulrich. *The Entrepreneurial Self: Fabricating a New Type of Subject*. London: SAGE, 2015.

Brown, Wendy. *States of Injury: Power and Freedom in Late Modernity.* Princeton NJ: Princeton University Press, 1995.

———. *Undoing the Demos. Neoliberalism's Stealth Revolution.* New York: Zone Books, 2015.

Bumiller, Kristin. *In an Abusive State: How Neoliberalism Appropriated the Feminist Movement against Sexual Violence.* Durham NC: Duke University Press, 2008.

Casarino, Cesare, and Antonio Negri. *In Praise of the Common: A Conversation on Philosophy and Politics.* Minneapolis: University of Minnesota Press, 2008.

Chozick, Amy. "Hillary Clinton Calls Many Trump Backers 'Deplorables,' and G.O.P. Pounces." *New York Times*, September 10, 2016.

Contratto, Susan. "A Feminist Critique of Attachment Theory and Evolutionary Psychology." In *Rethinking Mental Health and Disorder: Feminist Perspectives*, edited by Mary Ballou and Laura Brown, 29–47. London: Guilford, 2002.

Crenshaw, Kimberlé. "Demarginalizing the Intersection of Race and Sex: A Black Feminist Critique of Antidiscrimination Doctrine, Feminist Theory and Antiracist Politics." *University of Chicago Legal Forum* 1 (1989): 139–67.

———. "Mapping the Margins: Intersectionality, Identity Politics, and Violence against Women of Color." *Stanford Law Review* 43, no. 6 (1991): 1241–99.

Crépon, Marc, Barbara Cassin, and Claudia Moatti. "People/Race/Nation." In *Dictionary of Untranslatables: A Philosophical Lexicon*, edited by Barbara Cassin and translated by Emily Apter, Jacques Lezra, and Michael Wood, 751–64. Princeton NJ: Princeton University Press, 2014.

Dardot, Pierre, and Christian Laval. *Ce cauchemar qui n'en finit pas: Comment le néolibéralisme défait la démocratie.* Paris: La Découverte, 2016.

Davies, William. *The Limits of Neoliberalism: Authority, Sovereignty and the Logic of Competition*. London: SAGE, 2014.

Davis, Kathy. "Intersectionality as Buzzword." *Feminist Theory* 9, no. 1 (2008): 67–85.

Davis, Oliver. "Neoliberal Capitalism's Bureaucracies of 'Governance.'" In "Bureaucracy," edited by Jeremy Gilbert. Special issue, *New Formations* 100–101 (2020): 60–76.

———, ed. *Rancière Now: Current Perspectives on Jacques Rancière*. Cambridge: Polity Press, 2013.

Dean, Jodi. *Democracy and Other Neoliberal Fantasies: Communicative Capitalism and Left Politics*. Durham NC: Duke University Press, 2009.

Dean, Tim. *Beyond Sexuality*. Chicago: University of Chicago Press, 2000.

———. "The Biopolitics of Pleasure." *South Atlantic Quarterly* 111, no. 3 (2012): 477–96.

———. "Foucault and Sex." In *After Foucault: Culture, Theory, and Criticism in the Twenty-First Century*, edited by Lisa Downing, 141–54. Cambridge: Cambridge University Press, 2018.

———. "No Sex Please, We're American." *American Literary History* 27, no. 3 (2015): 614–24.

———. "Sex and the Aesthetics of Existence." PMLA 125, no. 2 (2010): 387–92.

———. *Unlimited Intimacy: Reflections on the Subculture of Barebacking*. Chicago: University of Chicago Press, 2009.

De Botton, Alain. *How to Think More about Sex*. New York: Picador, 2012.

Delany, Samuel R. *Times Square Red, Times Square Blue*. New York: New York University Press, 1999.

Deleuze, Gilles. "Desire and Pleasure." Translated by Daniel W. Smith. In *Foucault and His Interlocutors*, edited by Arnold I. Davidson, 183–92. Chicago: University of Chicago Press, 1997.

Dimen, Muriel. *Surviving Sexual Contradictions: A Startling and Different Look at a Day in the Life of a Contemporary Professional Woman.* New York: Macmillan, 1986.

Doyle, Jennifer. *Campus Sex, Campus Security.* South Pasadena CA: Semiotext(e), 2015.

Duggan, Lisa, and Nan D. Hunter. *Sex Wars: Sexual Dissent and Political Culture.* New York: Routledge, 1995.

Duschinsky, Robbie, Monica Greco, and Judith Solomon. "Wait Up! Attachment and Sovereign Power." *International Journal of Politics, Culture, and Society* 28, no. 3 (2015): 223–42.

Eng, David L., Judith Halberstam, and José Esteban Muñoz. "What's Queer about Queer Studies Now?" *Social Text* 23, no. 3–4 (2005): 1–17.

Epstein, Orit Badouk. "Working with the Incredible Hulk." In *Ritual Abuse and Mind Control: The Manipulation of Attachment Needs,* edited by Orit Badouk Epstein, Joseph Schwartz, and Rachel Wingfield Schwartz, 234–52. London: Karnac Books, 2011.

Epstein, Orit Badouk, Joseph Schwartz, and Rachel Wingfield Schwartz, eds. *Ritual Abuse and Mind Control: The Manipulation of Attachment Needs.* London: Karnac Books, 2011.

Fear, Rhona M. *Attachment Theory: Working Towards Learned Security.* London: Karnac Books, 2017.

Ferguson, Roderick A. *One-Dimensional Queer.* Cambridge: Polity Press, 2019.

Fischel, Joseph J. *Screw Consent: A Better Politics of Sexual Justice.* Oakland: University of California Press, 2019.

———. *Sex and Harm in the Age of Consent.* Minneapolis: University of Minnesota Press, 2016.

Foltz, Mary C. *Contemporary American Literature and Excremental Culture: American Sh*t.* London: Palgrave Macmillan, 2020.

Fontanel, Sophie. *The Art of Sleeping Alone: Why One French Woman Suddenly Gave Up Sex*. Translated by Linda Coverdale. New York: Scribner, 2013.

Foucault, Michel. *The Essential Works of Michel Foucault, 1954–1984.* Vol. 1, *Ethics: Subjectivity and Truth*. Edited by Paul Rabinow and translated by Robert Hurley. New York: New Press, 1997.

———. *The History of Sexuality*. Vol. 1, *An Introduction*. Translated by Robert Hurley. New York: Random House, 1978.

———. "An Interview by Stephen Riggins." In *Essential Works*, 121–33.

———. "Sex, Power, and the Politics of Identity." In *Essential Works*, 163–73.

Freud, Anna. *The Ego and the Mechanisms of Defence*. Translated by Cecil Baines. London: Karnac Books, 1993.

Freud, Sigmund. "Analysis Terminable and Interminable." 1937. In *The Standard Edition*, 23:209–53.

———. "The Antithetical Meaning of Primal Words." 1910. In *The Standard Edition*, 11:153–61.

———. *Beyond the Pleasure Principle*. 1920. In *The Standard Edition*, 18:1–64.

———. *Civilization and Its Discontents*. 1930. In *The Standard Edition*, 21:57–145.

———. "A Difficulty in the Path of Psycho-Analysis." 1917. In *The Standard Edition*, 17:135–44.

———. *Drei Abhandlungen zur Sexualtheorie*. 1904–5. In *Gesammelte Werke*, 5:27–145. Frankfurt: S. Fischer Verlag, 1942.

———. "The Dynamics of Transference." 1912. In *The Standard Edition*, 12:97–108.

———. *Five Lectures on Psycho-Analysis*. 1910. In *The Standard Edition*, 11:1–55.

———. "Instincts and Their Vicissitudes." 1915. In *The Standard Edition*, 14:109–40.

————. "Observations on Transference-Love." 1915. In *The Standard Edition*, 12:159–71.

————. *The Question of Lay Analysis: Conversations with an Impartial Person*. 1926. In *The Standard Edition*, 20:177–258.

————. *The Standard Edition of the Complete Psychological Works of Sigmund Freud*. Edited and translated by James Strachey. 24 vols. London: Hogarth, 1953–74.

————. *Three Essays on the Theory of Sexuality*. 1905. In *The Standard Edition*, 7:123–245.

————. "The Unconscious." 1915. In *The Standard Edition*, 14:159–204.

Gersen, Jacob, and Jeannie Suk Gersen. "The Sex Bureaucracy." *Chronicle of Higher Education*, January 6, 2017. http://www.chronicle.com/article/The-College-Sex-Bureaucracy/238805.

Gertner, Nancy. "Sex, Lies and Justice." *American Prospect*, January 12, 2015. http://prospect.org/article/sex-lies-and-justice.

Gottschalk, Marie. *The Prison and the Gallows: The Politics of Mass Incarceration in America*. Cambridge: Cambridge University Press, 2006.

Green, André. *The Chains of Eros: The Sexual in Psychoanalysis*. Translated by Luke Thurston. London: Rebus Press, 2000.

————. "Has Sexuality Anything to Do with Psychoanalysis?" *International Journal of Psycho-Analysis* 76 (October 1995): 871–83.

Hall, Donald E., and Annamarie Jagose, eds. *The Routledge Queer Studies Reader*. New York: Routledge, 2013.

Halley, Janet. *Split Decisions: How and Why to Take a Break from Feminism*. Princeton NJ: Princeton University Press, 2006.

Halley, Janet, Prabha Kotiswaran, Rachel Rebouché, and Hila Shamir. *Governance Feminism: An Introduction*. Minneapolis: University of Minnesota Press, 2018.

Halperin, David M. *Saint Foucault: Towards a Gay Hagiography*. New York: Oxford University Press, 1995.

Halperin, David M., and Trevor Hoppe, eds. *The War on Sex.* Durham NC: Duke University Press, 2017.

Hardt, Michael, and Antonio Negri. *Commonwealth.* Cambridge MA: Harvard University Press, 2009.

———. *Empire.* Cambridge MA: Harvard University Press, 2000.

———. *Multitude: War and Democracy in the Age of Empire.* New York: Penguin, 2004.

Harris, Jeremy O. *Slave Play.* New York: Theatre Communications Group, 2020.

Hayes, Peter. "Utopia and the Lumpenproletariat: Marx's Reasoning in *The Eighteenth Brumaire of Louis Bonaparte.*" *Review of Politics* 50, no. 3 (1988): 445–65.

Hazeley, Jason, and Joel Morris. *The Story of Brexit.* New York: Penguin Random House, 2018.

Herman, Judith. *Trauma and Recovery.* 2nd ed. New York: Basic Books, 1997.

Hinshelwood, R. D. *A Dictionary of Kleinian Thought.* 2nd ed. London: Jason Aronson, 1991.

Hofstadter, Richard. *The Paranoid Style in American Politics: And Other Essays.* New York: Knopf, 1965.

Holland, Sally. "Representing Children in Child Protection Assessments." *Childhood* 8, no. 3 (2001): 322–39.

Holmes, Jeremy. *John Bowlby and Attachment Theory.* 2nd ed. London: Routledge, 2014.

Jameson, Fredric. *The Political Unconscious: Narrative as a Socially Symbolic Act.* Ithaca NY: Cornell University Press, 1981.

Jenkins, Philip. *Moral Panic: Changing Concepts of the Child Molester in Modern America.* New Haven CT: Yale University Press, 1998.

Johnson, E. Patrick, and Mae G. Henderson, eds. *Black Queer Studies: A Critical Anthology.* Durham NC: Duke University Press, 2005.

Kahan, Benjamin. *The Book of Minor Perverts: Sexology, Etiology, and the Emergences of Sexuality*. Chicago: University of Chicago Press, 2019.

Kalifa, Dominique. *Les bas-fonds: Histoire d'un imaginaire*. Paris: Seuil, 2013.

Keyssar, Alexander. *Why Do We Still Have the Electoral College?* Cambridge MA: Harvard University Press, 2020.

Klein, Melanie. "Mourning and Its Relation to Manic-Depressive States." In *Love, Guilt and Reparation and Other Works, 1921–1945*, 344–69. London: Virago, 1988.

Lacan, Jacques. *The Four Fundamental Concepts of Psycho-Analysis*. Edited by Jacques-Alain Miller and translated by Alan Sheridan. Harmondsworth: Penguin, 1977.

Laclau, Ernesto. *On Populist Reason*. London: Verso, 2005.

Lacter, Ellen. "Torture-Based Mind Control: Psychological Mechanisms and Psychotherapeutic Approaches to Overcoming Mind Control." In *Ritual Abuse and Mind Control: The Manipulation of Attachment Needs*, edited by Orit Badouk Epstein, Joseph Schwartz, and Rachel Wingfield Schwartz, 97–216. London: Karnac Books, 2011.

La Fontaine, Jean. *Speak of the Devil: Tales of Satanic Abuse in Contemporary England*. Cambridge: Cambridge University Press, 1998.

Lamble, Sarah. "Queer Necropolitics and the Expanding Carceral State: Interrogating Sexual Investments in Punishment." *Law and Critique* 24, no. 3 (2013): 229–53.

Lancaster, Roger. "The New Pariahs: Sex, Crime, and Punishment in America." In *The War on Sex*, edited by David M. Halperin and Trevor Hoppe, 65–125. Durham NC: Duke University Press, 2017.

———. *Sex Panic and the Punitive State*. Berkeley: University of California Press, 2011.

Lane, Jeremy F. "Rancière's Anti-Platonism: Equality, the 'Orphan Letter' and the Problematic of the Social Sciences." In *Rancière Now: Current Perspectives on Jacques Rancière*, edited by Oliver Davis, 28–46. Cambridge: Polity Press, 2013.

Lapavitsas, Costas. *The Left Case against the EU*. Cambridge: Polity Press, 2019.

Laplanche, Jean. *Essays on Otherness*. Edited by John Fletcher. London: Routledge, 1999.

———. *Freud and the Sexual: Essays 2000–2006*. Edited by John Fletcher and translated by John Fletcher, Jonathan House, and Nicholas Ray. New York: International Psychoanalytic Books, 2011.

———. *Life and Death in Psychoanalysis*. Translated by Jeffrey Mehlman. Baltimore: Johns Hopkins University Press, 1976.

———. *The Temptation of Biology: Freud's Theories of Sexuality*. Translated by Donald Nicholson-Smith. New York: The Unconscious in Translation, 2015.

Laplanche, Jean, and J.-B. Pontalis. *The Language of Psycho-Analysis*. Translated by Donald Nicholson-Smith. New York: Norton, 1973.

Latour, Bruno. "Why Has Critique Run Out of Steam? From Matters of Fact to Matters of Concern." *Critical Inquiry* 30, no. 2 (2004): 225–48.

Levack, Brian. *The Witch-Hunt in Early Modern Europe*. 4th ed. London: Routledge, 2016.

Levine, Judith. "Sympathy for the Devil: Why Progressives Haven't Helped the Sex Offender, Why They Should, and How They Can." In *The War on Sex*, edited by David M. Halperin and Trevor Hoppe, 126–73. Durham NC: Duke University Press, 2017.

Leys, Ruth. *From Guilt to Shame: Auschwitz and After*. Princeton NJ: Princeton University Press, 2007.

———. *Trauma: A Genealogy*. Chicago: University of Chicago Press, 2000.

———. "The Turn to Affect: A Critique." *Critical Inquiry* 37, no. 3 (2011): 434–72.

Loftus, Elizabeth, and Jacqueline Pickrell. "The Formation of False Memories." *Psychiatric Annals* 25, no. 12 (1995): 720–25.

MacKinnon, Catharine A. *Feminism Unmodified: Discourses on Life and Law.* Cambridge MA: Harvard University Press, 1987.

———. "#MeToo Has Done What the Law Could Not." *New York Times*, February 4, 2018. https://www.nytimes.com/2018/02/04/opinion/metoo-law-legal-system.html.

———. *Sexual Harassment of Working Women: A Case of Sex Discrimination.* New Haven CT: Yale University Press, 1979.

Mansnerus, Laura. "For What They Might Do: A Sex Offender Exception to the Constitution." In *The War on Sex*, edited by David M. Halperin and Trevor Hoppe, 268–88. Durham NC: Duke University Press, 2017.

Marcuse, Herbert. *One-Dimensional Man: Studies in the Ideology of Advanced Industrial Society.* Boston: Beacon Press, 1964.

Marx, Karl. *The Eighteenth Brumaire of Louis Bonaparte.* [1852.] Translated by Daniel De Leon. New York: International Publishers, 1994.

———. "On the Jewish Question." In *Karl Marx: Early Writings*, edited and translated by T. B. Bottomore, 1–40. New York: McGraw-Hill, 1964.

Marx, Karl, and Friedrich Engels. *Manifesto of the Communist Party.* [1848.] Radford VA: Wilder Publications, 2007.

Mesli, Rostom. "Gayle Rubin's Concept of 'Benign Sexual Variation': A Critical Concept for a Radical Theory of the Politics of Sexuality." *South Atlantic Quarterly* 114, no. 4 (2015): 803–26.

Michaels, Walter Benn. *The Trouble with Diversity: How We Learned to Love Identity and Ignore Inequality.* New York: Henry Holt, 2006.

Miller, Peter, and Nikolas Rose. *Governing the Present: Administering Economic, Social and Personal Life.* Cambridge: Polity Press, 2008.

Moi, Toril. *Revolution of the Ordinary: Literary Studies after Wittgenstein, Austin, and Cavell.* Chicago: University of Chicago Press, 2017.

Mouffe, Chantal. *The Democratic Paradox.* London: Verso, 2000.

Mowitt, John. "Trauma Envy." *Cultural Critique* 46 (Fall 2000): 272–97.

Nancy, Jean-Luc. *Sexistence.* Translated by Steven Miller. New York: Fordham University Press, 2021.

Nash, Jennifer C. *Black Feminism Reimagined: After Intersectionality.* Durham NC: Duke University Press, 2019.

———. "Intersectionality and Its Discontents." *American Quarterly* 69, no. 1 (2017): 117–29.

Nelson, Dana D. *Bad for Democracy: How the Presidency Undermines the Power of the People.* Minneapolis: University of Minnesota Press, 2008.

———. *Commons Democracy: Reading the Politics of Participation in the Early United States.* New York: Fordham University Press, 2016.

———. "Democracy in Theory." *American Literary History* 19, no. 1 (2007): 86–107.

Nguyen, Tan Hoang. *A View from the Bottom: Asian American Masculinity and Sexual Representation.* Durham NC: Duke University Press, 2014.

Orwell, George. *Animal Farm.* London: Secker and Warburg, 1945.

Pape, Robert A., and Keven Ruby. "The Capitol Rioters Aren't Like Other Extremists." *The Atlantic*, February 2, 2021. https://www.theatlantic.com/ideas/archive/2021/02/the-capitol-rioters-arent-like-other-extremists/617895/.

Perrot, Michelle. "1848 révolution et prisons." *Annales Historiques de la Révolution Française*, no. 228 (1977): 306–38.

Phillips, Adam. *Equals.* New York: Basic Books, 2002.

———. *Unforbidden Pleasures.* New York: Penguin, 2015.

Puar, Jasbir K. *Terrorist Assemblages: Homonationalism in Queer Times*. Durham NC: Duke University Press, 2007.

Rancière, Jacques. *Disagreement: Politics and Philosophy*. Translated by Julie Rose. Minneapolis: University of Minnesota Press, 1999.

———. "The Fools and the Wise" (blogpost). Translated by David Fernbach. Verso, January 22, 2021. www.versobooks .com/blogs/4980-the-fools-and-the-wise.

———. *Hatred of Democracy*. Translated by Steve Corcoran. London: Verso, 2014.

———. *The Ignorant Schoolmaster: Five Lessons in Intellectual Emancipation*. Translated by Kristin Ross. Stanford CA: Stanford University Press, 1991.

———. *La haine de la démocratie*. Paris: La Fabrique editions, 2005.

———. *The Philosopher and His Poor*. Translated by John Drury, Corinne Oster, and Andrew Parker. Durham NC: Duke University Press, 2003.

———. *The Politics of Aesthetics: The Distribution of the Sensible*. Translated by Gabriel Rockhill. 2nd ed. London: Bloomsbury, 2013.

Ricoeur, Paul. *Freud and Philosophy: An Essay on Interpretation*. Translated by Denis Savage. New Haven CT: Yale University Press, 1970.

Rodríguez, Juana María. *Sexual Futures, Queer Gestures, and Other Latina Longings*. New York: New York University Press, 2014.

Rouvroy, Antoinette, and Thomas Berns. "Algorithmic Governmentality and Prospects of Emancipation: Disparateness as a Precondition for Individuation through Relationships?" Translated by Elizabeth Libbrecht. *Réseaux* 177, no. 1 (2013): 163–96.

Rubenstein, Diane. *This Is Not a President: Sense, Nonsense, and the American Political Imaginary*. New York: New York University Press, 2008.

Rubin, Gayle S. "Blood under the Bridge: Reflections on 'Thinking Sex.'" In *Deviations: A Gayle Rubin Reader*, 194–223. Durham NC: Duke University Press, 2011.

——. "Thinking Sex: Notes for a Radical Theory of the Politics of Sexuality." In *Pleasure and Danger: Exploring Female Sexuality*, edited by Carole Vance, 267–319. London: Routledge, 1984.

Saketopoulou, Avgi. "The Draw to Overwhelm: Consent, Risk, and the Retranslation of Enigma." *Journal of the American Psychoanalytic Association* 67, no. 1 (2019): 133–67.

——. "Risking Sexuality beyond Consent: Overwhelm and Traumatisms That Incite." *Psychoanalytic Quarterly* 89, no. 4 (2020): 771–811.

——. *Risking Sexuality beyond Consent: Race, Traumatophilia, and the Draw to Overwhelm*. New York: New York University Press, forthcoming.

Salecl, Renata. *A Passion for Ignorance: What We Choose Not to Know and Why*. Princeton NJ: Princeton University Press, 2020.

SAMOIS, ed. *Coming to Power: Writings and Graphics on Lesbian S/M*. 3rd ed. rev. Boston: Alyson, 1987.

Schuster, Aaron. *The Trouble with Pleasure: Deleuze and Psychoanalysis*. Cambridge MA: MIT Press, 2016.

Schwartz, Rachel Wingfield. "'An Evil Cradling?' Cult Practices and the Manipulation of Attachment Needs in Ritual Abuse." In *Ritual Abuse and Mind Control: The Manipulation of Attachment Needs*, edited by Orit Badouk Epstein, Joseph Schwartz, and Rachel Wingfield Schwartz, 74–96. London: Karnac Books, 2011.

Scott, Darieck. *Extravagant Abjection: Blackness, Power, and Sexuality in the African American Literary Imagination*. New York: New York University Press, 2010.

Sedgwick, Eve Kosofsky. *Epistemology of the Closet*. Berkeley: University of California Press, 1990.

————. "Paranoid Reading and Reparative Reading, or, You're So Paranoid, You Probably Think This Essay Is about You." In *Touching Feeling: Affect, Pedagogy, Performativity*, 123–51. Durham NC: Duke University Press, 2003.

————. *Touching Feeling: Affect, Pedagogy, Performativity*. Durham NC: Duke University Press, 2003.

Shapira, Michal. *The War Inside: Psychoanalysis, Total War, and the Making of the Democratic Self in Postwar Britain*. Cambridge: Cambridge University Press, 2013.

Sinason, Valerie. "How Do We Help Ourselves?" In *Trauma and Attachment: The John Bowlby Memorial Conference Monograph 2006*, edited by Sarah Benamer and Kate White, 83–92. London: Karnac Books, 2008.

————. "What Has Changed in Twenty Years?" In *Ritual Abuse and Mind Control: The Manipulation of Attachment Needs*, edited by Orit Badouk Epstein, Joseph Schwartz, and Rachel Wingfield Schwartz, 17–73. London: Karnac Books, 2011.

Sinason, Valerie, and Robert Hale. *Pilot Study on Alleged Organised Ritual Abuse: Final Report*. 2000. Accessed April 19, 2019. https://www.whatdotheyknow.com/request/389624/response /969467/attach/4/REDACTED%20REPORT.pdf.

Spade, Dean. *Normal Life: Administrative Violence, Critical Trans Politics, and the Limits of Law*. Durham NC: Duke University Press, 2015.

Stallybrass, Peter. "Marx and Heterogeneity: Thinking the Lumpenproletariat." *Representations* 31 (Summer 1990): 69–95.

Stockton, Kathryn Bond. *Beautiful Bottom, Beautiful Shame: Where "Black" Meets "Queer."* Durham NC: Duke University Press, 2006.

Storr, Will. "The Mystery of Carole Myers." *The Observer: Mental Health*, December 11, 2011. https://www.theguardian.com/society /2011/dec/11/carole-myers-satanic-child-abuse.

Suleiman, Susan Rubin. "Judith Herman and Contemporary Trauma Theory." *Women's Studies Quarterly* 36, no. 1–2 (2008): 276–81.

Theweleit, Klaus. *Male Fantasies.* Vol. 2, *Male Bodies: Psychoanalyzing the White Terror.* Translated by Erica Carter and Chris Turner. Minneapolis: University of Minnesota Press, 1989.

Thompson, E. P. *Customs in Common.* London: Merlin, 1991.

Tomkins, Silvan. *Shame and Its Sisters: A Silvan Tomkins Reader.* Edited by Eve Kosofsky Sedgwick and Adam Frank. Durham NC: Duke University Press, 1995.

Treichler, Paula A. *How to Have Theory in an Epidemic: Cultural Chronicles of AIDS.* Durham NC: Duke University Press, 1999.

Tuck, Richard. *The Left Case for Brexit: Reflections on the Current Crisis.* Cambridge: Polity Press, 2020.

Tuhkanen, Mikko. *The Essentialist Villain: On Leo Bersani.* Albany: State University of New York Press, 2018.

Van der Horst, Frank, and René van der Veer. "Separation and Divergence: The Untold Story of James Robertson's and John Bowlby's Theoretical Dispute on Mother-Child Separation." *Journal of the History of the Behavioral Sciences* 45, no. 3 (2009): 236–52.

Van der Kolk, Bessel. *The Body Keeps the Score: Brain, Mind, and Body in the Healing of Trauma.* New York: Penguin, 2014.

———. "The John Bowlby Memorial Lecture 2006: Developmental Trauma Disorder; A New, Rational Diagnosis for Children with Complex Trauma Histories." In *Trauma and Attachment: The John Bowlby Memorial Conference Monograph 2006,* edited by Sarah Benamer and Kate White, 45–60. London: Karnac Books, 2008.

Van der Kolk, Bessel, and Mark Greenberg. "The Psychobiology of the Trauma Response: Hyperarousal, Constriction, and Addiction to Traumatic Reexposure." In *Psychological Trauma,* edited by Bessel van der Kolk, 63–87. Washington DC: American Psychiatric Press, 1987.

Van Dijken, Suzan. *John Bowlby: His Early Life*. London: Free Association Books, 1998.

Van Rosmalen, Lenny, and Frank van der Horst. "From Secure Dependency to Attachment: Mary Ainsworth's Integration of Blatz's Security Theory into Bowlby's Attachment Theory." *History of Psychology* 19, no. 1 (2016): 22–39.

Virno, Paolo. *A Grammar of the Multitude: For an Analysis of Contemporary Forms of Life*. Translated by Isabella Bertoletti, James Cascaito, and Andrea Casson. Los Angeles: Semiotext(e), 2004.

Warner, Michael. "Queer and Then?" *Chronicle of Higher Education* 58 (January 1, 2012): B6–B9.

Watney, Simon. *Policing Desire: Pornography, AIDS and the Media*. London: Methuen, 1987.

Whyman, Philip B. *The Left Case for Brexit: Active Government for an Independent UK*. London: Civitas, 2018.

Wiegman, Robyn. *Object Lessons*. Durham NC: Duke University Press, 2012.

Wittgenstein, Ludwig. *The Blue and Brown Books*. Oxford: Basil Blackwell, 1958.

Yellin, Judy. "Such Stuff as Dreams Are Made On: Sexuality as Re/creation." In *Sexuality and Attachment in Clinical Practice: The John Bowlby Memorial Conference Monograph 2004*, edited by Kate White and Joseph Schwartz, 21–58. London: Karnac Books, 2007.

Zupančič, Alenka. *What Is Sex?* Cambridge MA: MIT Press, 2017.

To order or obtain more information on these or other University of Nebraska Press titles, visit nebraskapress.unl.edu.

"Fascinating, formidable, and timely, this volume probes unexpecte
links between democracy and sexuality. *Hatred of Sex* will undoubtedl
disturb established ideas that are widely and at times too reflexivel
adopted in current academic conversations about sexuality. A manifest
grounded in careful scholarship, this book has the makings of a classic.
—**AVGI SAKETOPOULOU**, faculty of the Postdoctoral Program in Psycho
therapy and Psychoanalysis at New York University

"*Hatred of Sex* is a bold critical intervention. . . . No other book has offere
such an unapologetic and persuasive critique of the incursion of ant
democratic and sex-hating discourses in queer theory. Davis and Dea
make arguments that few others would dare to wage."—**JOHN PAUL RICCO**
professor of comparative literature at the University of Toronto

Hatred of Sex links Jacques Rancière's political philosophy of the constitutiv
disorder of democracy with Jean Laplanche's identification of a fundament
perturbation at the heart of human sexuality. Sex is hated as well as desire
Oliver Davis and Tim Dean contend, because sexual intensity impedes coherer
selfhood and undermines identity, rendering us all a little more deplorable tha
we might wish. Davis and Dean explore the consequences of this conflicte
dynamic across a range of fields and institutions, including queer studies, attach
ment theory, the #MeToo movement, and "traumatology," demonstrating ho
hatred of sex has been optimized and exploited by neoliberalism.

Advancing strong claims about sex, pleasure, power, intersectionality, ther
apy, and governance, Davis and Dean shed new light on enduring questions o
equality at a historical moment when democracy appears ever more precariou

OLIVER DAVIS is a professor of French studies at the University of Warwic
He is the author of *Jacques Rancière* and editor of *Rancière Now*. **TIM DEAN**
James M. Benson Professor in English at the University of Illinois at Urban
Champaign. He is the author of *Unlimited Intimacy: Reflections on the Subcultu
of Barebacking* and *Beyond Sexuality*.

UNIVERSITY OF NEBRASKA PRESS
LINCOLN NE 68588-0630
NEBRASKAPRESS.UNL.EDU

ISBN 978-1-4962-3059-1